CHRISTMAS - AND ALWAYS

Rita F. Snowden is widely known in many countries and is the author of more than sixty books for adults and children. After six years at business she trained as a deaconess of the New Zealand Methodist Church, serving in turn two pioneer country areas before moving to the largest city for several years of social work during an economic depression.

Miss Snowden has served the world Church, beyond her own denomination, with regular broadcasting commitments. She has written and spoken in Britain, Canada, the United States, in Australia, and in Tonga at the invitation of Queen Salote. She has represented her church at the World Methodist Conference in Oxford; later being elected the first woman Vice-President of the New Zealand Methodist Church, and President of its Deaconess Association. She has been an Honorary Vice-President of the New Zealand Women Writers' Society, and is a Fellow of the International Institute of Arts and Letters, and a member of P.E.N.

Miss Snowden has been honoured by the award of the Order of the British Empire, and by the citation of "The Upper Room" in America.

A prolific writer, her books include *A Woman's Book of Prayers*, *More Prayers for Women*, *Bedtime Stories and Prayers* (for children), and *Sharing Surprises*.

D0206402

CHRISTMAS – AND ALWAYS

Rita Snowden

Collins
FOUNT PAPERBACKS

First published in Great Britain by
Fount Paperbacks, London in 1989
Second impression February 1990

Copyright © Rita Snowden 1989

Printed and bound in Great Britain by
William Collins Sons & Co. Ltd, Glasgow

*Carrying my love
to the many readers
of
my many books*

CONTENTS

FOREWORD

This book – as you will soon see – like life itself is, for the most part, a happy thing! It is in the nature of celebrations that it should be so – Christian celebrations especially!

There may have been minor celebrations, of course, before the Christian era – before the world was properly out of its "swaddling clothes"! Related, perhaps, to birth, growth and harvest!

But of one thing I am sure: there was then no woman writer to be spurred on by bright publishers, to sit down and produce yet another book. There were indeed no books! In time, there were chiseled stone slabs and parchments, but they were all very limited! Aèons of time had to pass, before even the Book of Genesis was put together!

* * * *

So we will let this little row of "stars" stand for all that we *don't* know of that dim, early occasion – and never shall know! Life must have been unbearably dull without books, and I am glad that I wasn't given life, and born to grow up, then!

* * * *

Let this second little row of "stars" stand for all those unfortunates who *were* given life in those slow-moving centuries, the years until you and I, separately, could each sit down with a *lap full of books to enjoy – this one among them!*

Though, between its two covers, it doesn't tell us exactly *how* to celebrate. We will each have our own ideas about that, largely depending, I think, on which part of this great round world we live in, man or woman, and whether or not we belong to Christ's ongoing Church. It has been my lot to travel with a widely-serving task, keeping my eyes open, and now here, as I write, I lay hold of some precious realities others have celebrated – and many still do!

This second day of the second month of the year, as I write, is often, here in New Zealand, a golden sunny day. But it is no longer a special day in the life of the Church, as it used to be in many parts of the world way back in the Middle Ages when February the Second welcomed in "Candlemas Day", celebrating the Purification of the Virgin Mary, and the Presentation of the Babe Jesus in the Temple!

So, it was a very important day. In time, it also became the day for the blessing of church candles, many of which were lit and then carried in procession around the church.

But nowhere, at least, as far as I know, is it important today – save where in some places it is kept as "Scottish Quarter Day", a time for settling certain accounts. Its religious nature has been *lost*!

R.F.S.

Waiting With Eagerness

ADVENT

I did not know the word "Advent" when I was a child. The Christmas word I first learned – not its spelling, but to hold in my heart with joy – was the word *expecting*. It was such an eager word, and real! Whenever I saw our father take his spade and rake, softening the soil in a certain corner of the garden, and answering, when Mother put in an appearance: "Yes, I was *expecting* to have some this season," I clapped my hands. A day would come, I knew, when we would have strawberries, and be called away from our play to help pick them. We liked that!

And there was that other time, when Mother unwrapped a soft parcel she had brought home from Town with her, and said, when she saw the twins' eyes upon her: "I'm *expecting* to make 'you two' new woolly nighties for the Winter."

And there was that day when, out walking, we came upon a neighbour who said to our Mother: "I didn't know that Mrs Bloomfield was 'expecting'. Did you?" As I overheard, I felt that something good must be going to happen. And it did – after nine months!

A long time later, when I was old enough to hold up a hymnbook all by myself in chapel, it was Christmas again soon, and I heard them sing, what I later learned was Charles Wesley's hymn:

Come Thou *long-expected Jesus*,
  Born to set Thy people free,
From our fears and sins release us,
  Let us find our rest in Thee.

I knew by then that some kinds of *expecting* took a long time – but I was growing up, and a student by correspondence, studying books that would later help me with my New Testament exams, at "Methodist Deaconess House". It was then that I came across an author, Dr J. Paterson Smyth, with lots of letters behind his learning, telling of Christ's coming that first Christmas, and writing of it so happily, so clearly.

"One cannot but feel," said he in his opening, "that *here we are in an atmosphere of tense expectation*". (And I've kept a copy of that enlightening book on my study shelves ever since, no longer shy of his many letters: DD, LLD, LittD, and DCL, never questioning his wisdom, nor ceasing to be grateful for it. Unhappily, not all learned authors, I found, had the gift of putting profound things into lucid English. (I'm afraid that it must be now but a second-hand copy of his book, *A People's Life of Christ*, that must content you in any bookshop if you look for one, and I can't be sure even of that.)

The message of the old prophets, as he said, "grew into a definite hope, a growing expectancy, but it wasn't an easy event. For, in an historical way, *three races* were involved! And Christmas could never have come to our world without them!"

A century before Christ's coming, the world was

very broken up, localized, subdivided, with separate little peoples, bristling frontiers, and minor wars. "Humanly speaking", a century before Christ no Palestinian movement could ever have spread beyond Palestine, no universal Gospel have won free course throughout the world.

But just at this crisis, came a striking change. When Jesus came, instead of frontiered nations separated and suspicious, He found a levelled world. **Rome** *had welded the incoherent kingdoms* into one great monarchy, *the Roman roads* traversed the civilized world; and the iron power of the Caesars *kept universal peace*. The highway was open for the coming of the King. So far the Romans.

And what of **the Greeks**? An open road for the Gospel would have been of little avail, *without a common language* to carry it through the world. (The Jew spoke Aramaic, the Roman knew Latin, the many other peoples spoke languages as confused as at Babel.) But as the day drew nearer when Messiah was coming, the Greek, all unknowing, was doing his part to prepare "the way of the Lord". His beautiful, flexible tongue became the chief language of the Empire, for people all round the Mediterranean, while speaking their own language, also learned to use Greek. It became the language of the whole civilized world. Thus the vehicle was prepared for carrying the new teaching. How else, we may well wonder, could Paul and his colleagues have successfully accomplished their wide missionary journeys, and thus made possible the establishment of the Early Church?

An expectant Faith was also essential – and this **the Jew** had! Historians find joy in telling us how, through forward-looking prophecies of Old Testament times, this was done. With Christ's birth in Bethlehem, made possible in humble circumstances, this became known to the world as God's action, in time! As now we celebrate it! Our parents, preachers, teachers and poets lead us in rejoicing as to how it was done. And where!

* * * *

Richard Crashaw, poet and priest, helped English folk to rejoice in its reality away back between 1612 and 1645. And his words quicken our hearts still:

Welcome! All Wonders in one sight!
Eternity shut in a span,
Summer in Winter, day in night,
Great little One! Whose all-embracing birth
Lifts earth to heaven, stoops heav'n to earth!

* * * *

In our day, Neville Cardus rejoiced to tell how, in Lancashire and Yorkshire, "*The Messiah* is never produced except at Christmas. We always," said he, "begin practising *The Messiah* in the first week of December. We never call it 'rehearsing'. The choir-master who led us was Herbert Lomas – who worked at the loom in a neighbouring mill. He was the product of the celebrated Old English custom of the 'Half-timer' – a custom which allowed children to go into the mills at six in the morning – afterwards to school at midday, after a morning's hard labour calculated to stimulate the intellect – and get it ready for an afternoon of education in the 'Board' Schools of the period.

"Like many other Lancashire and Yorkshire men, he was self-taught in music, and in most other things of the mind and spirit. He used a tuning fork, and he would strike it and tell us to keep in tune. 'Now then, lads and lassies,' he would say, 'fill thi chests with air, and put some guts into t' singin'. Listen to me, all you basses, tha' don't mak' half eno' row. Why, dang me, dost'n not remember that owd Handel when he composed th' Alleyllolyer chorus saw th' 'eavens open and all t' angels and the Lord 'Isself? I don't suppose any of you chaps 'll ever see t' angels in 'eaven if tha' doesn't tak' this opportunity. So let thiself go, every one on ye! And thee, 'Arry Pearson, when tha' sings t' tenor air, "T' trumpet shall sound", open thi' mouth and let's hear thi. Come on, lad. Why, I've 'eard thi mak' more noise when tha's been appealin' for leg-before against t' Wigan second eleven.'

"And he would strike his tuning fork again, and we would all make a humming sound. Then Herbert would begin beating time with his stick. Sometimes he would stop us suddenly, leaving George Watson, the local greengrocer, entirely exposed on a sustained note in his chest register."

* * * *

For young, and old, there is always something special in a Christmas celebration. There is a wonderful "expectancy", as John recorded simply, and unforgettably, in his Gospel: *"The Word became flesh, and dwelt among us!"* (John I:14, A.V.).

And the true spirit of "Advent" is in "getting ready *to receive Him anew in one's whole spirit, mind, and body! Here, and now! In this very World into which He came!*

* * * *

One sings with wonder:

> I know not *how* that Bethlehem's Babe
>   Could in the God-head be;
> *I only know the Manger-Child*
>   *Has brought God's Life to me!*

(Anon)

* * * *

Surely, no one sharing this modern life – with its millions within the world Church (and without) has better set down for us, what here and now we need to celebrate, than Dr J. Robert Oppenheimer. Many have sought to hear what they might from an atomic scientist, and here are his telling words concerning one Christmas certainty, whilst speaking of the worth of an exchange of students of different countries. In his summing up he said: *"The best way to send an idea, is to wrap it up in a person!"* (It doesn't come out of the New Testament – ever close to life – but it very well might!)

For that's precisely what God did at Bethlehem! He wrapped His greatest idea in a person – a very tiny person – and laid Him in a manger. Eleanor Farjeon, English poet of our day, gave glory to God for it, and shared it widely – especially where there were children.

> Just before bed,
> "Oh, one more story,
> Mother!", they said;
> And in the glory
> Of red and gold
> Beyond the fender
> Their Mother told
> Splendour on splendour.
>
> "Don't stop, Mother!"
> "It's time to rest."
> "Oh, tell us Mother,
> The very best!"
> So the best of all
> She told to them:
> *"Once in a stall*
> *In Bethlehem . . ."*

★   ★   ★   ★

Our Prayer

> Gracious God, this is a glorious Day! Guide our
>   hearts to the very centre of its celebration!
> Save us from being too taken up with *things*,
>   with pretty ones, or costly ones!
> As we sing our carols, and delight in our
>   decorations,

keep us, young and old, close to the wonder
of Thy Son,
Our Saviour, the Christ Child!

R.F.S.

* * * *

ONCE, NOW, AND EVERMORE!

Much More than X-Mas

FOR CELEBRATION ANYTIME!
It began, of course, away back in the Heart of God
Himself, as it could not have done anywhere else —
not even in the lively imagination of a child, or the
world travel plans of us "Pilgrims". Bethlehem was
God's wonderful idea, as was everything that went
with it, save Herod! (I think that he and his plans
could only have originated with the Devil — as did
Hitler and his plans, centuries on, in the same fiendish
killing of innocent little ones.) Any old faded newspaper you might uncover by chance in an attic, will
persuade you of that evil deed. Christmas called for
more than any Earth-dweller could conceive. *And it
does still!* Even Little Jo's idea, in Louisa May Alcott's
story *Little Women*, had limitations: "Christmas," said
she, "wouldn't be Christmas, without presents!" (But
that's little more than the idea of the advertiser
and the toyshop manager, set on keeping the till
bell tinkling!) *"Christmas", more truly, gladly, "is
not Christmas without Christ!"* And presents, stock-
ings and pretty decorations come a long way after.
Christmas is a glorious Birthday — and ever must be!
  One wise grownup asks:

What can a mother give her children
    Greater today than this one great thing,
Faith in an old, sweet, beautiful story,
    A Star, a stable, a newborn King?

Shining faith in the young lad, Jesus:
   Lover of high, fine things, was He;
Jesus – straight as a Lebanon cedar,
   Jesus – clean as the winds from the sea!

As children, it's fun to have fairy stories early – but they can never hold a lasting place in our hearts. If we learn of Ali Baba and the Forty Thieves we must later learn the true story of Jesus crucified between two thieves! If we liked Little Red Riding Hood, surprisingly meeting the Wolf, much more will we love the real story of two tired travellers, meeting Jesus – risen from the dead, alive again forever, walking with them to their home in Emmaus. And at the end of the journey going in to share a meal with them (Luke 24:13–52, A.V.). *One of our world's greatest real stories!* If we could not know its Reality, Life would be very different! If today we could not each declare gladly, with our friends:

He is not far away:
Why do we sometimes seem to be alone,
And miss the hands outreached to meet our own?
He is the same today,
As when of old, He dwelt with His disciples
   – when He knew the needs of all His fellow men,
   And all their sorrows felt.
   Only our faith is dim,
So that our eyes are holden, and we go
All day, and until dusk, before we know
   That we have walked with Him.

Henry Lyte, the gifted hymnwriter, wove this

certainty into what Dame Clara Butt called "The World's Loveliest Hymn: *Abide with me!*" He had based it on the invitation of those two with whom Christ walked the Emmaus Road: They constrained Him, saying, "*Abide with us: for it is toward evening, and the day is far spent. And he went in to tarry with them*" (Luke 24:29).

* * * *

All this began at Bethlehem years before – as the New Testament says – "The Word became flesh, and dwelt among us" (John 1:14).

John Betjeman, in our day, introduces one who asks —

And is it true? And is it true,
  This most tremendous tale of all,
Seen in a stained-glass window's hue,
  A Baby in an ox's stall?
The Maker of the stars and sea
Became a Child on earth for me?

I have been to Bethlehem – and I say *"Yes! Yes! Yes!"*
And in many other places where He left His footprints, I say *"Yes! Yes! Yes!"* And in my New Testament study page (2 Corinthians 5:19) I read with the given authority of Heaven and Earth: "God was in Christ, reconciling the world unto Himself . . ." adding a verse from further on: "Now then, we are ambassadors for Christ." Not even The New English Bible can make it more plain: when the translation says: "What I mean is, that God was in Christ reconciling the world to Himself . . . and

that He has entrusted us with the message of reconciliation."

Whilst in Bethlehem, I sought out a high spot overlooking the Shepherds' Field, where those humble working men minded sheep, and I took time to read again the New Testament story of what they experienced there. Without loss of time, that very night, they saw *a Babe cradled in a nearby Manger — following the Angels' Song; and instructions to seek Him out!* Was ever greater cause for celebration? And this is what we rejoice to do, in our own way, *year by year*, when we set our eyes toward Bethlehem!

* * * *

Dr John Baillie, the beloved Scottish preacher of our day, said: *"Let us ascribe unto the Father and unto Christ the Son all honour and glory and merit throughout all ages, world without end."*

* * * *

Dr W. R. Maltby (my longtime friend of Ilkley Deaconess College), after an exchange of visits to each other's countries, and of books, talks and letters) rejoiced to refer to the event of Bethlehem — "The Incarnation" — as *"The greatest thing done on Earth!"* And that's saying a great deal! Another able preacher friend of exchange visits, books, and talk, celebrating Christmas from his London pulpit, one year unforgettably exclaimed: "Listen! *He stepped out of Bethlehem!* Here is the glorious truth of it: 'The Word became flesh and dwelt among us . . . No man hath seen God at any time; the only begotten

Son, which is in the bosom of the Father, He hath declared Him.'

"Christianity is not just a religion of influence, and values, and principles. *It is,*" added my friend, "*a religion of happenings; of events; of historical occurrences . . . It belongs to the very marrow of the Gospel to assert that God came at a certain hour in history, and at a certain place on earth; lived and died among us, and afterwards rose from the dead.*"

"The man who says, 'I cannot believe that. I admire the ethics of the Sermon on the Mount, and much of the teaching of Christ, but the *historical* part of it, I find incredible' – that man or woman," says my preacher friend, "might be many splendid things, but he or she could not be a believer in the Christian religion. *The Christian Religion carries certain facts at its heart, and the greatest of them is: 'The Word became flesh, and dwelt among us!'* " (John 1:14).

* * * *

Bethlehem is more, much more, than a mother's story to tell children at Sunday School, or sitting on the hearthrug at home! It is in itself more than a pleasant place to spend an afternoon in congenial company, a few miles out of Jerusalem – though it is that too. My home-sharing friend and I found it so, and I will always be thankful for that. We were in Jerusalem for a week and had lodging with Christian friends, and it was not far to spend time together in little Bethlehem which we did twice that week. This was my *first* time in Bethlehem, but for the missionary friend showing us round, it was her *last* in a lifetime of service that she had loved. The years had given her more, she assured us, than many friends, and an honourable retirement.

That Sunday afternoon, under another's leadership, we went to visit a little company of blind children — to tell them stories, and share cold fruit drinks, and to listen to them sing. When they learned that Rene and I had come from our home on the other side of the world, and could understand English words, the children sang to us the only little song that they knew "in English" — one that *our* own small Sunday School children sing, at Christmas. They took Phillips Brook's simple words, and they sang, in their little piping voices, their unseeing eyes raised high.

> *O little town of Bethlehem,*
>> *How still we see thee lie!*
> *Above thy deep and dreamless sleep*
>> *The silent stars go by;*
> Yet in thy dark streets shineth
>> The everlasting Light;
> The hopes and fears of all the years
>> Are met in thee tonight.
>
> How silently, how silently
>> The wondrous gift is given!
> So God imparts to human hearts
>> The blessings of His heaven.
> No ear can hear his coming;
>> But in this world of sin,
> Where meek souls will receive Him, still
>> The dear Christ enters in.

Here we were *in* little Bethlehem – where *in the heart of it, still*, His daily, caring, "shepherding" was being lovingly done!

★　★　★　★

Morning Prayer

Gracious Father of us all, we would seek now, and ever, new meanings, and more loving qualities in our daily "comings and goings". We would give thanks for good men and women, away back to Mary and Joseph, in tender parenthood.

Bless this day all who set up "caring homes" – however simple. Establish within, we pray, sincere trust and loving, lasting respect. In sickness and in health, hold us in Thy keeping.

Bless, and strengthen especially, all who find in their daily tasks the need for lively patience and purpose. Set a song upon their lips, too, from day to day; and some living beauty about them.

Bless all little ones, for whose coming, just now Life provides but "a lowly crib", akin to that of the Little Lord Jesus in Bethlehem. We ask for these lovely, everlasting, holy gifts in His Name; and for His Kingdom's sake.　　AMEN.

R.F.S.

And Such a Star!

EPIPHANY

Though there is no one living now who saw it, countless millions among us, the whole world round, know it for truth – and love to think about it. Matthew wrote of it joyously in his Gospel, though for some reason, real enough no doubt, when they were writing, none of the evangelists did. The Star appeared above Bethlehem, a quietish little town still (Matthew 2:1–12; A.V.). I have known its story by heart ever since I got my first New Testament, but I never dreamed then that one day I would take that book out and read it as I stood overlooking Bethlehem. Matthew wrote:

> In the days of Herod the king, behold, there came Wise Men from the east, to Jerusalem, saying: "Where is He that is born King of the Jews? For we have seen His star in the east, and are come to worship Him!" When Herod the king had heard these things, he was troubled, and all Jerusalem with him.
>
> And when he had gathered all the chief priests and scribes of the people together, he demanded of them where Christ should be born. And they said unto him, "In Bethlehem of Judaea: for thus it was written by the prophet, 'And thou Bethlehem, in the land of Juda, art not the least among the princes of Juda; for out of thee shall come a Governor, that

shall rule my people Israel.' "

Then Herod, when he had privily called the Wise Men, enquired of them diligently what time the star appeared. And he sent them to Bethlehem, and said, "Go and search diligently for the young child; and when ye have found him, bring me word again, that I may come and worship him also." When they heard the king, they departed: and, lo, the star, which they saw in the east, went before them, till it came and stood over where the young child was. When they saw the star, they rejoiced with exceeding great joy. And when they were come into the house, they saw the young child with Mary His mother, and fell down, and worshipped Him; and when they had opened their treasures, they presented unto Him gifts; gold, and frankincense, and myrrh.

And being warned of God in a dream that they should not return to Herod, they departed into their own country another way.

* * * *

Interest in the Wise Men has been sustained through the centuries, but the New Testament, for all that, does not tell us how many of them there were. We assume their number was *three* because of their three gifts – Gold, Frankincense and Myrrh – precious, all of them, and suitable for a young King! Gold was counted a rich gift – the king of metals! Frankincense for a princely person associated with worship, and sacrifice. Myrrh a suitable offering for one who is to die. Holman Hunt, the artist, has a famous picture of our Saviour, Jesus, showing Him as a youth against the door of the carpenter's workshop in Nazareth, holding up his arms outstretched, because they have become cramped – the setting sun casting a shadow *in the form of a cross!* In the background stands Mary, His mother, deeply absorbed! (A symbol – as were those three gifts offered to Him as a babe by the Magi!)

★ ★ ★ ★

The most telling celebration I have experienced was in London, at a Service that concerned the Queen, though she was not herself present in person. It was held in one of the small chapels. "Go to the Chapel Royal a few minutes before eleven o'clock, and there will be a seat for you," said a receptionist when I called at the appropriate office some days earlier, to ask whether I might attend.

On the day before the Feast of the Epiphany, a small package had been carried from London's oldest pharmacy in St James's Street, to the office of the Lord Chamberlain. It held *two ounces of frankincense, and two ounces of myrrh*, to which would be added, when the moment came, twenty-five golden sovereigns – the Queen's offering.

I found my seat silently, thoughtfully. The small Chapel, lacking any stained glass, which usually gives colour to such occasions, suddenly quickened into glorious life with the arrival of the Yeomen of the Guard, in their Tudor scarlet-and-gold, and with the Queen's Chaplain, in his scarlet. Hymns, prayers, and Scripture reading recalled the original giving of

The Three Wise Men!

Then we heard the strains of the Carol, *Whence is this goodly fragrance?*, as two people advanced to offer the precious gifts, on the Queen's behalf.

Those of long ago, of whom Saint Matthew wrote, had, of course, *no deputy*. Nor have we, in presenting what gifts we have to Christ, our Lord. And with such thoughts stirring, I moved out into London's crowded life once more, as the celebration closed.

* * * *

Tertullianus, Quintus Septimius Florens (a fine fistful of names he carried, away back in the years 160–230). As one of the earliest Christian theologians, he claimed to be the *first* to be able to give the Three Wise Men their names: Caspar, Melchior and Balthazar. (In our farming part of the world, I met them first, in their borrowed robes, with golden cardboard crowns, as "Mr Palmer, Mr Evans, and the farmboy, Tom, as they came together up the church aisle, singing: *We three Kings of Orient, are!* One year, they all had beards!)

When we twins were about seven, there were not many children came to church at night – it was a long way to go, in the trap – and when we got there it was "all sort of hushed", like proper church. The big people seemed to like it – but then, it was only once a year. It wasn't really "a children's thing", so I was all but grown-up, when I heard of "a celebration", with a good sprinkling of children present. One little boy had a loudly-whispered question he wanted answered, about "The Three Guys"! It's not easy to forget such questions, is it, given childhood's fresh innocence? Our "country shyness" saved us, most times, I expect.

T. S. Eliot, our modern day poet, has widely identified himself with that early hazard of the Wise Men. He is ready to credit them with unbelievable courage. You may be familiar with his lengthy poem, *Journey of the Magi*, but I hope I may be granted copyright permission to quote here, where it fits so well, its beginning:

> A cold coming we had of it,
> Just the worst time of the year
> For a journey, and such a long journey;
> The ways deep and the weather sharp,
> The very dead of winter.
> And the camels galled, sore-footed, refractory,
> Lying down in the melting snow.
> There were times we regretted
> The summer palaces on slopes, the terraces
> And the silken girls bringing sherbet.
> Then the camel men cursing and grumbling
> And running away, and wanting their liquor and
>   women,
> And the night fires going out, and the lack of
>   shelters,
> And the cities hostile and the towns unfriendly
> And the villages dirty and charging high prices:
> A hard time we had of it.

But it wasn't for nothing — wearied though they must have been, in time, they were bowing lowly, presenting gifts, and with their hearts full of wonder!

After the Star, the dim day,
After the Gifts, the empty hands,
And now we take our secret way
Back to far lands.
After the Joy, the weary ride,
But journey we, *three new-made men*
Side by side!

T. S. Eliot

From time to time, at this season of the year, my steady friend *Anonymous* will offer me something fresh. (But I've no idea where to send him a letter of thanks – I wish I did.) Today, it's a seasonal prayer that fits perfectly into this page:

Blessed art Thou, O Christmas Christ,
   that Thy cradle was so low that shepherds,
poorest and simplest of all earthly folk,
   could yet kneel beside it,
and look level-eyed into the face of God.

* * * *

My Morning Prayer
Eternal God, revealed in Christ the Child, lent to this World; I rejoice in Thy Holy Love, and Thy power and presence in my life, this day. I rejoice in the Scriptures, mercifully presented to me in my own language. For the long-time service of this world's scholars and saints, I bless Thee!

For Christian friendship, and the supportive experience of travel, in this wide and wonderful world of Thy making, I bless Thee. As I do daily, for home, and Church, for books, and music ever varying, and challenging and enriching!

Hold, day by day, in Thy merciful keeping, O Lord,
all who have few opportunities, and limited gifts
and graces, all with frail bodies yet with the work-
time need to "hustle and bustle". All bearing daily,
heavy responsibilities, all linked with uncongenial
workmates.

Give them Love to share, and Patience, and keep
their judgements generous and kind and keen! And
at all times — through Church, work and home —
let them serve Thy Kingdom!

AMEN.

R.F.S.

* * *

God in the Highest — let Catherine Baird's words
challenge us at this particular time of celebration:

What profit, should we win the race,
To solve the mysteries of space,
To signal through ten thousand nights,
If we neglect to read the Star
Shining forever from afar,
Of Jesus, cradled from His birth
On the dark bosom of the Earth?
And what are victories of skill
Unless exploring in God's will,
We prove the Law we there have found
In this our world — our holy ground?

Close to Christmas

BOXING DAY

Season by season, it has long been my pleasure to spend these two special days, Christmas Day and Boxing Day, in the home of dear friends. We have known each other since far away student days, and when they married, I was their very *first* home guest. (As we recall, they explained, "We felt we could practise on you!", which I took as a nice compliment!) Along with their parents, I have looked forward to these two days at the beginning of each year, and nothing, short of travel overseas, has broken in on the sequence.

On Boxing Day, we also remember with another chuckle, how later their young son, Tony, broke in on adult conversation to ask, "Daddy, when do we go to see the Boxers?"

★　★　★　★

There was a little explaining to do, but as I've gone about, I've noticed how few adults can give a child an explanation of the name *Boxing Day*. I was fortunate myself, early on, to find it whilst seeking an answer for something else, in *The Book of Days*. Lately, when "a bookish friend" lent me her set — two monster volumes, rare these days — I saw that it had been published in 1888, exactly a century earlier. Under the date for Boxing Day, I seized on the subheading: "CHRISTMAS BOXES", and read that, at the time of its writing, "it could be said: 'Christmas boxes are still regularly expected by the postman, the lamplighter, and the dustman, and generally expected by all those functionaries who render services to the public at large, without receiving payment therefor from any particular individual' " (p. 765). But it did find room, in its packed columns of small type and long sentences, for a report that "this custom of Christmas boxes – even yet to a certain extent – continues to be *a great nuisance*". Though in another statement, it suggested that the custom had its origin "in the times of the ancient Romans".

* * * *

Life, of course, has changed very greatly since then. We have now, as a matter of historical fact, *no* unpaid postmen or dustmen, and no lamplighters at all of the old sort, save for a practice in London, as an historic link, of tending the lamps around The Temple Church, set beneath its beautiful trees. (And I hope it will long remain.) There by happy chance one evening, waiting to meet a friend, I suddenly saw the old lamplighter approaching. We met at one of the many remaining lamp standards, beneath the soaring trees. Seeing my interest he stopped, and placed his tall wand in my hand, with the query: *"You would like to light it?"*

So it was, that there – holding my breath a moment – I stood on tiptoe, and reaching up, lit a little light high up, in the oncoming darkness, glad that old London still likes to remember an ancient event!

But with us, Boxing Day no longer carries its early meaning; and for many in our midst, no particular meaning at all, much less a fitting Christian association with St Stephen, the first Christian martyr, and his supreme self-giving! So this day does not call them to celebration of any sort.

★ ★ ★ ★

"Thy martyr Stephen" The New English Bible of our day renders as "Thy *witness* Stephen". And it may be a good thing, sounding to us a little less remote. We are not much acquainted with "martyrs" – but we are close to "witnesses". (And up through the centuries, the two words, in the early languages, have brought them "shoulder to shoulder".)

For the fullest meaning of both, we can't here do better than turn up our New Testament Book of Acts and read through Stephen's story in Chapter 7, following any part of Stephen's "Apology", you have read in the previous pages by way of introduction – till you come to his fearless words in verse 51. Thereafter "witness" and "martyrdom" are forever mingled costingly!

To this day, in many parts of our world, there are spiritual realities bringing change of a dramatic kind. The young man whom we came in time to call "Paul", was present when Stephen gave up his life – minding the spare clothes of those hurling stones at Stephen so that they might more terribly do the job!

Never for a moment did anyone looking on guess that a day would come when Augustine would find himself saying to the whole world of his time: "The Church owes Paul to the prayer of Stephen!" (Acts 7:60). He was a man close to his Risen Lord!

This is the spiritual quality of the man we celebrate on 26th December!

★   ★   ★   ★

When I was in Jerusalem, I purposely sought out and mounted the slope to St Stephen's Gate, which the Orthodox Church regards as the scene of the stoning of Stephen.

Other pilgrims prefer what seems to them a more likely location, at St Stephen's Church, north of the city wall. Who, at this date, after the disturbances of centuries, could be certain? Enough to say, that on an earthly spot, within this old city, heroic Stephen – first martyr of the Christian Church, to which we now belong – gave up his life, witnessing to our common Lord! In many cities of the world today, churches bear his name – including an early one in our pioneer city of Auckland, by the sea. Little more than a chapel in size – but beautifully built, and through long years tended lovingly by staff and members of the Anglican Cathedral. It was my privilege, some years back, there to lead a Quiet Day for the women of the Cathedral. And I shall never forget it – the morning air sweet about us as we reverently entered, the surrounding lawn mown that very morning, the little Chapel looking out to sea!

It is good on Boxing Day, wherever we are, and of whatever section of the world Church, to keep fresh in our hearts the Witness of St Stephen!

And may it remind us of the living words of Augustine: *"The Church owes Paul to the prayer of Stephen."*

Let us read again the appropriate passage, from the New Testament Book of Acts 7:54–60 (A.V.): "And he kneeled down, and cried with a loud voice: 'LORD, LAY NOT THIS SIN TO THEIR CHARGE.'

"And when he had said this, he fell asleep."

★ ★ ★ ★

Prayer

O God, before whose face the generations rise and pass away, we rejoice *in the communion of the saints.* We remember all who have faithfully lived, all who have peacefully died . . . May it please Thee to give us at last a place with those who have trusted in Thee, and striven to do Thy holy will.

And to Thy Name, thrice holy, with the Church on earth, and the Church in heaven, would we ascribe all honour and glory, world without end. Amen.

From *Divine Worship* (Approved for optional use, in Methodist Churches, 1958. Eighth impression.)

"For the young person in your family," I once wrote in a book of mine, *OVER THE DOORSTEP*, "what is your greatest wish?" "The greatest ambition I have for my boy," said Dr Roger Lloyd, *"is that he should meet a saint."*

Surprising? No, not at all. Just proof that this good modern father is not as silly as some, and knows what he really means by a saint. He is not thinking of an ascetic with thin feet in sandals and his head in a halo.

"It is impossible to measure," wrote Professor Butterfield, in his widely read *Christianity and History*, "the vast difference that ordinary Christian piety has made to the last two thousand years of European history!" Not all were martyred like Stephen, fortunately – but all were *faithful witnesses*!

God's idea of a saint, as I understand it in this challenging world in which we find ourselves, is no poor, pale person of pious resignation – far from it. *Rather, in God's eyes a saint is a strong, much-involved character of Christian rejoicing and wonder!*

★   ★   ★   ★

Our Thanksgiving Here and Now
O God, we thank Thee for the dear and faithful dead, who have made the distant heavens a home for us. One by one, Thou dost gather the scattered families out of earthly light into heavenly glory, from the distraction and strife and weariness of time, to the peace of eternity. We thank Thee for the labour and joy of these mortal years, for the mysteries that lie beyond our dust, and for the hope that enters within the veil. Gather us at last with those who by faith and patience inherit the promises; through Jesus Christ our Lord.   AMEN.

From *Divine Worship*

A Loved Hymn to Share
  For all the saints who from their labours rest,
  Who Thee by faith before the world confessed,
  Thy name, O Jesus, be for ever blest,
    Allelulia!

  O blest communion, fellowship divine!
  We feebly struggle; they in glory shine,
  Yet all are one in Thee, for all are Thine.
    Allelulia!

Every struggle for freedom, every lonely stand for the right, all sacrifice, all heroism, has never been made in vain. It is the high price valiant hearts must pay for a better world. Their willingness is a mark of their belief. They believe it is God's world, and that if the foundations of the New Order have to be laid on the bones of the brave, and through toil and tears, it may, after all, be the process through which God teaches us true peace, true brotherhood, and right values. *Whatever happens, they know and are persuaded.*

                              Norman N. G. Cope

A Good New Year!

STARTING AGAIN

We are Earth people – so wherever celebrations take us, it's good to keep close to God's good Earth! And this is especially so on this day unlike any others He gives us: the first day of a New Year! Its first secret, I fully believe, lies in learning to "travel light"!

Just over a hundred years ago, an official *Guide to the North-Western Railway* made its appearance in England. One section of it was headed: "Hints for Starting", and its first words read amusingly: "A traveller should decide whither he is going." (Surely!) "By what railway train, and when. Then, whether he will have to change carriages at any point, and where." (It sounds very innocent.)

Further on, this important point is advanced: "The traveller is advised to take *as little luggage as possible*; and ladies are earnestly entreated not to indulge in more than *seven* boxes and *five* small parcels for the longest journey." (Really?) Surely, no lady could feel herself deprived with that allowance. Unless she was moving house, and not just going to visit Aunt Annie for a day or two.

* * * *

In these modern times we all travel – whether to see friends at the far end of the country, or on the other side of the world! (I have myself done the last-named thing nine times now, in "book service", with *stops* and *starts* in between, by ship or by plane. It's not simple, for all that it generally adds up to be "enjoyable". The ever present fact is that for big bags, and a little one with the documents one needs to show – diary, with dates and times, and passport, and purse, etc. – *one has only one pair of hands*, and again and again, in a surging crowd, no time to spare. And this is not the end – there are right exit doors to go through, when the surging, excited column breaks up and, if the weather is unwelcoming, raincoat and umbrella to attend to – ALL WITH ONE PAIR OF HANDS!

It's not so simple, even at the ninth time – because by the time one has returned HOME, it has become the EIGHTEENTH TIME! (One needs a husband, good natured and strong as an elephant, or a welcoming friend, to bring a car, a smile, and *two more hands to the situation!* Without them, world travel today – even for an experienced woman – is hard work. When I see the immaculately uncrumpled gulls, in their white and silver-grey, whirling overhead as we land, I envy them – that they have no problem of luggage!

★ ★ ★ ★

"When our Lord sent out His disciples on their first experimental campaign of evangelism," Dr Erik Routley reminds us today, "He emphasized this necessity of *travelling light.*"

Palestine, the area that they were going to cover, was not large in our terms as I discovered on my own feet, with but a haversack as luggage. Only a hundred and forty miles long, and narrow — with more added for the trans-Jordanic uplands. But the surfaces were rough in those days. A proverb widely known then said: "There are three states of misery — sickness, fasting, and *travel*." Before a traveller set out upon a journey, he was advised "to pay his debts, provide for dependants, give parting gifts — *and bid farewell to all*." Mark 6:8–9, in our Revised Standard Version, gives us the Master's words, in our own language: "He charged them to take nothing for the journey except a staff, no bread, no bag, no money in their belts, but to wear sandals and not put on two tunics."

An early traveller, Thomas Hearne — suffering from having a good deal of his luggage stolen — wrote of his *apparent* misfortune: "The weight of our baggage being so much lightened, our next day's journey was *so much more swift and pleasant.*"

★   ★   ★   ★

The Latin word for *baggage* is generally accepted as *impedimentum*, and its challenge to us modern disciples — literally, and spiritually — is to stop and consider how many things, *even good things*, can become an impediment.

There exists our very human, but no less foolish, addiction to carrying many *bad* things as well at the centre of our personality — fears, grudges, and angular, awkward chunks of human pride. There is no doubt that in every way, we travel better when we *travel lightly*. It's something well worth learning.

★   ★   ★   ★

Dr Nathaniel Micklem of our own day, knowing us well, within the world Church facing this New Age, accepts with The New Testament challenge. "The Kingdom of Christ," he says, "*must be ready to leave behind* much of its past, its order, and its ideas." (I wonder?)

One of the new hymns from *WITH ONE VOICE*, the newest Hymn Book it is my joy to own, and meant for all the churches as it claims to be, offers the following by Colin Alexander Gibson (1933–), embracing only Christian essentials for our close consideration, that of serving Christ:

He came singing *love*
And He lived singing *love*;
He died, singing *love*.
He arose in silence.
For the *love* to go on
We must make it *our* song;
you and I be the singers.

2. He came singing *faith* . . .
3. He came singing *hope* . . .
4. He came singing *peace* . . .

* * * *

A Morning Prayer (Perhaps to memorize, at least in part)
Gracious Lord, I hush my heart to ponder these essentials of Your Kingdom. Hear me, I humbly pray. And enable me to cast off all that is a hindrance in my discipleship.

I do not ever need to pretend in Your presence — but rejoice to speak those things I can utter to no other.

I want to begin this new, unspoiled day with eagerness; and with Love to end it — pleasing You, my Eternal Father.

Forgive me, if ever I am so busy that others cannot tell me of their troubles; or in any high moment, feel free to share it with me.

I am thankful that You draw no line, at any time, between things sacred and things secular — since all are Your gifts to my life.

Let me value always Your supportive Love, and kindly providence. In the Name of Your Son — Christ, my Saviour — I ask it.   AMEN.

R.F.S.

* * * *

An Evening Prayer

O God, this day which was Thy gift has come to its close, and I pause to give thanks for it. Starting with *good things* . . . I can share with those dear to me.

Not forgetting *unexpected things* — which also often bear Your mark. Forgive me now, for any cross word spoken; any prideful word; any word untrue.

Forgive me, if this day I have passed, *unconcerned*, any that I might have helped in any way — by kindly action or encouraging word. Keep me mindful that in this part of the world the "Jericho Road" still runs — with its hurt, and its help, and its Christ-like ministry of "Good Samaritans" —

unlikely looking though some of them are. From time to time, let me find myself, humbly, amongst their number. For the Sake of my Master, Christ, Who has shown me how to serve.   AMEN.

R.F.S.

★ ★ ★ ★

A Waking Prayer, for Both Young and Old
Lord, teach me how to "travel light" this day – in the Spirit of my Master, I pray – and for his sake.   AMEN.

★ ★ ★ ★

A Prayer to Add to One's Own, Here and Now
(Written in our day, in this world we all share, by the late Dr Harry Emerson Fosdick – a loved American minister and author)

Set our feet on lofty places;
Gird our lives that they may be
armoured with all Christ-like graces
in the fight to set men free.
Grant us wisdom,
Grant us courage,
That we fail not men, nor Thee.

(Read it slowly – till you understand what every line means for you – in your life. When the time comes you can be sure that God will answer your prayer with something so much better than anything done on this Earth all by yourself. Try it, and see! *The Master, Christ, will surprise you, if you give Him a chance.*)

GOOD TRAVELLING! KEEP AT IT!
THERE'LL BE LOTS TO CELEBRATE.

★ ★ ★ ★

A Beginners' Prayer – Use it when you can find a quiet spot

O God, it is good to be alive, and here – though it's hard to wait to do all the things I want to do.

You have made the world so "rich", so great, so crammed full of possibilities – and so beautiful, in many of its sounds and shapes.

I thank You for all who have given me this chance to learn, and to be happy: my family, my teachers, my friends!

Let me show a proper respect for things that have come to me out of others' toil, and their steady, patient trying.

Establish my values – and let my body, mind and spirit each have its full part in what is clean, good and joyous!

In odd moments of temptation, let me not lower my standards. But, depending on Your mighty strength, and loving guidance known to others before me, win through. Enrich my friendships, enliven our fun; and give us a genuine concern for others less fortunate, this world round. AMEN.

R.F.S.

Deep Joy

CELEBRATING A GLORIOUS SECRET

Mid-morning, as I planned to pass through a new country town, where my friend Paul ministers, I meant to pause for a few minutes' chat, but he was not at home. His wife, Phyl, came to the door, all smiles, to say, "No, I'm sorry; he's not at home. Will you step in? I don't think he'll be long now. But then, I never really know – *he's gone to another wedding!*"

"I expect he gets a good many, in this newish place," I said. "Yes," she replied. "They seem to know that Paul likes weddings and is good at them – and cares very much how the young people get on in their new venture into life. He likes it to be joyous!"

"Exactly!" was the only thing I could think of to say, as I rose. "Well, tell him I called." And with that, she saw me settled at the wheel again, to go on with the rest of my journey. As I assembled thoughts of my brief visit, I felt glad that in this busy modern world – as ever – there's nothing human ever outside the interest of Jesus, our Lord of Life. And I fell to thinking, as the miles spun by, how striking it was, that the first engagement that opened His public ministry, was a *wedding*, as told in the New Testament, in the little community of Cana of Galilee! (For many of us who would like to turn up the record, it's easily found, in the beginning of John's Gospel: chapter 2:1–11.) One thing about it stands out – *it was a joyful occasion!* The Law exempted a bridal party from the burden of "fasting".

Jesus likened His relationship to His disciples, and theirs to each other, to a bridal party – I think, with a smile playing about His eyes. Hospitality of heart and mind He enjoyed so much! John the Baptist knew nothing of this, for he fasted, and ate sparsely. Not so Jesus – He was a *Man of Joy. Real Joy!* (The world, He knew, held both sunshine and shadow. For him, they were to culminate in a Cross – but it was in his Father's world, so He accepted both.)

Jesus's joy went deep – far deeper than friends, work, and fortuitous events – for it was part of His very nature; and He liked to share it. Fittingly, Paul – after whom my young minister friend was named – wrote in a letter (1 Timothy 6:17) *"God giveth us richly all things to enjoy."* (Paul, in prison for his faith at the time of writing, lacked much – yet this was his triumphant word to his young friend, Timothy, setting out on his Christian service. A prison in those days, as Paul was obliged to know, was a testing situation.) The old Westminster Divines, in time, were right to catch up on this Christian witness with the words: *"Man's chief end* is to glorify God, *and to enjoy Him forever"* (*The Shorter Catechism*).

* * * *

My long-time writer friend Dr Frank Boreham and I enjoyed serving the same English publishing house, "The Epworth Press", a dream of John Wesley's lively mind and spirit, and one that carries into the wide world, the name of his birthplace, EPWORTH.

Boreham and I were both solitary writers – save for the postbox – pursuing a distant ministry through words far from each other, one in Australia, the other in New Zealand. And each of us many thousands of miles from our publisher in London! So, we met only once, in all our writing years, and that was in Melbourne, when I crossed by air, to fulfil a series of speaking engagements. Late one afternoon, we met over a pot of tea, my friend accompanied by his wife and two charming teenage daughters. It was good fun, and we all enjoyed it! But we two writers were not as free to talk books as perhaps we might have liked. My friend had just written another book in which was a story I liked. It concerned someone who, in the Rocky Mountains, had come upon an old Roman Catholic priest, frail, awkward, and tottering – but pressing on. Asked politely, "What are you doing, Father?" the old priest replied, *"I'm seeking out the beauty of the world!"*

"But," queried the man, gently, "have you not left it rather late?"

It was then that the old priest told him his story. All his life had been lived in a monastery – he had hardly set foot outside it. One night, he was very ill, and during his illness, he had a vision. An angel stood beside him. "What have you come for?" asked the old priest. "To lead you home," said the angel. "Is it a very beautiful world to which I go?" "It is a very beautiful world from which you come," said the angel. "And then," said the old priest, "I remembered that I had seen nothing of it, save the fields and the trees round the monastery. So I said, "I have seen very little of the world I am leaving." "Then," said the angel, "I fear you will see very little beauty in the world to which you are going." "I was in trouble," said the old man, "and I begged that I might stay for two more years. My prayer was granted, and I am spending all my little hoard of gold, and all the time I have, in exploring the world's loveliness. *And I find it very wonderful!*"

★   ★   ★   ★

"I did not press on *to enjoy my God,*" said Augustine, in a moment of deep regret, and referred to it as a great loss. He would be one to feel that this is something we ought to do – but naturally, and *freely choose to do so all our days!*

We can see that it will take us all the rest of our lives, to know fully all that it means! "If you turn over the pages of Wesley's *Journal*," one of his ministers of our modern day, the Rev. James Mackay, of Priory Methodist Church, Doncaster, wrote eagerly, in his charming little book, *Shaken Mists*, "you will be amazed at the hours he spent in prayer and meditation. But through that acute fixing of his attention upon God, the very Spirit of God mingled with his own spirit, until he found a serenity that nothing could ruffle, a courage nothing could daunt, a gaiety that made him one of the most attractive persons ever given to the world. Both his power, and his charm came from his enjoyment of God."

* * * *

Prayer

O God, we thank Thee for this universe, our great home; for its vastness and its riches, and for the manifoldness of the life which teems upon it, and of which we are a part. We praise Thee for the arching sky and the blessed winds, for the driving clouds, and the constellations on high. We praise Thee for the salt sea, and the running water, for the everlasting hills, for the trees, and for the grass under our feet.

We thank Thee for our senses, by which we can see the splendour of the morning . . . Grant us, we pray Thee, a heart wide open to all this joy and beauty, and save our souls from being steeped in care, or so darkened by passion that we pass heedless and unseeing when even the thornbush by the wayside is aflame with the glory of God.   AMEN.

(And thanks to Dr W. Rauschenbusch, for allowing us freely to share his prayer.)

* * * *

Said Dr Harry Fosdick in his book *The Manhood of the Master*:

What do we call real joy? Jesus enjoyed nature and friendship and social life, and so should we. Jesus loved good health, and spent much of His time healing the bodies of men. Jesus loved the best reading at His disposal, and was perfectly at home in the prophets. All his joys were fine and high.

Without going deeper into the distinctly religious sources of Jesus's joy, examine your own heart.

The simplest sights He met —
The sower flinging seed on loam and rock;
The darnel in the wheat; the mustard tree
That hath its seed so little, and its boughs
Widespreading; and the wandering sheep; and nets
Shot in the wimpled waters – drawing forth
Great fish and small – these, and a hundred such,
Seen by us daily, never seen aright,
Were pictures for Him from the page of life,
Teaching by parable.

>   By an unknown author – quoted in
>   *Cliffs of Opal* by F. W. Boreham, D.D.

Said Christ: "These things have I spoken to you, that *My joy* may be in you, and that *your joy* may be full" (John 15:11; R.S.V.).

And again: "So you have sorrow now, but I will see you again and your hearts will rejoice, and *no one will take your joy from you*" (John 16:22; R.S.V.).

These were not the easy words of a well-wisher – but parting words of Jesus to his disciple friends, as He was about to finish a known, bodily relationship and begin another – just as real, though unseen. They found it so – as you and I do today!

★　★　★　★

Behind this joyous book – the New Testament – and the joyous religion of Jesus, our Risen Lord, stands *His joyful Personality*.

The mournful pictures of Him in medieval art are proved wrong by the records of His relationship with His true followers in the world, to this hour. (I have read many of their triumphant life stories, and met many of them in person! I hope you have, too.)

* * * *

"He had the most joyous idea of God, that ever was thought of," wrote Dr Harry Fosdick, in his lively study book, *The Manhood of the Master*, at a most important time for me, when I was growing up. To this day, I feel sorry for any young person, beginning to lay hold of life's values, who does not somehow meet with an attractive Christian character, either at home, school, church, college, or club. Or meet with a book that will do for him or her what *The Manhood of the Master* did for me. It was an exciting find!

To finish Dr Fosdick's quotation: "He taught His disciples that they could take the most beautiful aspects of human life, like fatherhood, and lifting them up to the best they could imagine, could say, 'God is much better than this.' 'If ye then, being evil,' He said, 'know how to give good gifts unto your children, *how much more* shall your Father?' (Matthew 7:11, A.V.).

"This is the most joyous thought of God," concluded our helper, Dr Fosdick, *"of which we know!"*

Glory Be to God!

WHILE WE SHARE WORSHIP

Now, it seems impossible, but in far away days, it was so: nowhere, amidst the homes of the people, did a church spire arise, for there were no church buildings at all! And no full-time preachers, trained, and set aside to the ministry. Any news of the Gospel came by letter, to little knots of courageous Christians, gathered here and there in modest houses. And the letter did not come by post, for there was no such thing. Letters came at very long intervals and uncertain times, dependent upon some known Christian, or a trusted friend, who chanced to be travelling. Written by Paul, for the most part, and addressed to someone in some distant place – "Greet Priscilla and Aquila, my helpers in Christ Jesus, who have for my life laid down their own necks . . . Likewise greet *the church that is in their house*" (Romans 16:3, 5). At another time, "Paul, a prisoner of Jesus Christ, and Timothy our brother, unto Philemon our dearly beloved, and fellow labourer. And to our beloved Apphia, and Archippus our fellow soldier, and *to the church in thine house*" (Philemon, verse 2). And so on it went – references scattered amongst the Epistles of the New Testament. Men and women, many of them assembled for worship and instruction, by night, slinking along darkened back streets. It was a courageous thing to do and they did it continually.

What an exciting thing it is now, to leaf through
the New Testament we possess in safety, looking
for all those words: *"the church which is in thine house."*
But so was the Gospel shared, and Christian witness
spread!

★ ★ ★ ★

A home isn't often the setting today, which is why
I value the more a simple experience that came to
me, during a lengthy itinerary of preaching in widely
scattered places in England, some time ago. And I still
treasure it.

I had never been in that country part of the
north before. "Pott Yeats", the spready Christian
farmhouse, which would have delighted Paul, stood
on a steepish hillside. On the Sunday I was there, we
worshippers made our way from various parts of the
dale.

Methodist services, I learned, had been held in
the old farm kitchen every Sunday afternoon since
1864, and that was a long time back – to when the
Grandfather and Grandmother of the family first
started farming at "Pott Yeats".

Many of the sincere, country folk present before
me that Sunday, as I rose to lead worship, had been
christened under that kindly roof; many had made
there the most precious Christian discoveries of their
lives.

Paul, in the first century, would have understood
what such an experience meant to them. He understood the rich content of that phrase: *"the church which
is in thine house."*

More chairs were brought in, and Aunt Nan
Huddleston took her place at the little organ. Forty-
one folk crowded into the old kitchen, and three
"made the best of things" on the steps outside.

In time, our Service began, and all were welcome
– as welcome as those Christians of the first century.
And, as in the first century, *One Who blessed them, was
in our midst!*

★ ★ ★ ★

Worship Today is as Important as Ever
    The Kingdoms of the Earth go by
        In purple and in gold:
    They rise, they flourish, and they die,
        And all their tale is told.
    One Kingdom only is divine,
        One banner triumphs still:
    *Its King a servant, and its throne
        A Cross upon a Hill.*

                                        Anon

There is no need to modernize a fifth-century collect:
    Bless all who worship Thee
        From the rising of the sun
    Unto the going down of the same.
        Of Thy goodness, give us,
    With Thy love, inspire us . . .
        By Thy Spirit, guide us;
    By Thy power, protect us;
        In Thy mercy, receive us;
    Now and always, Amen.
                                        Anon

My Morning Prayer, on Rising

Gracious God, my Father, I rejoice, that safe and
  sound, I welcome in the day.

I bless Thee for the beauty of the world about me,
  for the colours of the sky, grass, and gardens.

For the fields spread out, and the fruitfulness of trees.
  I bless Thee for the life of friendly creatures;

But most of all, I give Thee thanks for kindly
  fellow men,
    and for the trust of little children, and the shared
      experience of middle age, and maturity.

And for all the gentleness of a womanly touch.
  At every turn, we know Thy wonderful Care
    – and Rejoice.   Amen.

                                                    R.F.S.

* * * *

Evening Prayer

Gracious Father, for all the elderly, lonely, and
  unsure, I pray. Especially, those known to me
  by name —— and ——.

Let the sacredness of human life come home to
  me afresh tonight. And bless, I pray Thee, all
  who labour to lighten the lot of others.

Bless this night, O Lord, all those newly literate,
  I pray; all who prepare books and stories suitable
  to their capacity.

Support, too, all those who spend their days pre-
  paring talking books. And all who use other
  modern means of bringing the wonder and meaning of the world to those long denied – the blind,
  and the deaf.

Bless now, with a plentiful supply of books, all
those with ample time for reading in their old age,
or in days of physical indisposition. And grant a
blessing on all those who serve through libraries,
I pray.   Amen.

R.F.S.

*　*　*　*

"The Word," said John, *"became flesh, and dwelt
among us*, and we beheld his glory, the glory as
of the only begotten of the Father, full of grace
and truth"* (John 1:14; A.V.).

Exactly! And we give ageless thanks for it. Love
is no longer a glory in the heavens, it skips alongside its Mother, going to the well to draw water for
household needs; it picks up, and handles a plane in
a carpenter's workshop; it walks with sandalled feet
the dusty ways of life; it stretches out a hand to
the distraught, and blesses little children. It kneels
to remove sandals, and to wash the dusty feet of
quarrelsome disciples; it chases animals out of God's
House of Worship!

> I know not *how* that Bethlehem's babe
>   Could in the Godhead be;
> I only know the Manger Child
>   Has brought God's life to me.
>   Anon

Asked, in an international camp, how her church
folk managed to spread the Good News of God,
Maria answered: "Oh, we don't have missions or give
away pamphlets. We just send one or two Christian

families to live and work in the village, and when they see then what Christian families are like, they want to be Christians, too." (Is that how you and I witness to our Faith?) *It is the way of Bethlehem* – an idea wrapped up in a Person!

★ ★ ★ ★

Commenting on what she had learned from her New Testament record of Mary and Joseph's Nazareth home, Evelyn Underhill's words are:

> We see the new life growing in secret. Nothing very startling happens. We see the Child in the carpenter's workshop. He does not go outside the frame of the homely life in which He appeared. It did quite well for Him, and will do quite well for us . . . for the pressure of God's Spirit is present everywhere . . . Our environment itself, our home and our job, is the medium through which we experience the moulding of His besetting love.

★ ★ ★ ★

Canon Raven's words concerning our modern Christian home are just as striking: "Love binds us in a fellowship that is perpetually enlarged."

Of some home-lovers, someone wrote unforgettably: "They were not well-dressed; their shoes were far from being waterproof. But they were happy, well pleased with one another, and contented with the time."

★ ★ ★ ★

The present generation, it seems, has always bothered some of us. Said one outspoken gentleman: "The young people of today think of nothing but themselves. They have no reverence for parents, or old age. They are impatient of all restraint. They talk as if they knew everything; and what passes for wisdom with us, is foolishness to them." "As for the girls," adds this observer with decided views, "they are forward and immodest, and unwomanly in speech, behaviour, and dress."

Well, he has a command of words – and perhaps brings to your uncomfortable consideration some known to us today, racing wildly about the countryside, on the backs of motor cycles, or at the wheel of some sleek little car!

(But perhaps, before you enjoy your judgement on those young folk, too freely – I ought to mention that all this was originally penned by one called Peter, a monk, *in 1274!*)

* * * *

In quest of something better to share, I jumped the next few centuries, till I came to John Wesley. More than most, he moved about continually. And what had he to say? Let me tell you: "It is very hard that neither a sense of duty, nor all my thundering from the pulpit, can persuade young ladies and gentlemen to visit a poor person in the finest summer evening; while those very same delicate and time-loving young people will spend a whole night in dancing, which must be an exercise equal to walking

Glory Be to God!

many miles" – and, I would add: "Attending several Sunday's Worship Services!"

* * * *

Gracious Companions

ARBOR DAY

Tucked into his small cane crib, our baby brother was daily set out of doors for his morning sleep beneath trees. My twin sister and I were probably treated in the same manner, some years before, but by the time I came to the moment of wanting to verify this, all three who could have told me – Father, Mother and only brother – had already "gone upon their way".

But of one thing I can be thankful: our farm-house hill and river surroundings *graced our lives with trees!* And all my days I have loved them, as being among God's good gifts, and have felt many of my experiences made beautiful by them. They contribute very much to the fact that my little country is a welcomingly "green country".

Arbor Day is, as far as I know, nowhere treated as a religious celebration, but well it might be, since its "graciousness" comes from God. From the start, it was a day set aside for tree planting in Nebraska, America, way back in 1872. The idea has spread, and now, year by year, it is widely welcomed in my own home country. Its date is printed yearly in my little red pocket diary that goes with me everywhere, just in case I should forget and be sorry. However, Arbor Day is such that I'm never likely to forget it, nor are other keen tree lovers, the world round. The actual Day – as *Everyman's Encyclopaedia* is at pains to remind us, is made known "by proclamation". There are seasonal reasons for that. From devoting one hour to the planting of a single tree in order to beautify public grounds, it has gradually become the great occasion for impressing on schoolchildren, and all present, the importance of forestry, and the actual planting of seedling trees to re-forest waste lands. And there are many of these, worldwide.

Trees are now such a part of the life of us all that we cannot live responsible lives if we forget that fact.

Deprived of trees, the earth might still be rock, sand, desert or vast icelands. It is within the power of trees to give the earth fertility. Rain falls, branches and leaves break the force of fierce storms, and water runs gently to the earth, filtering through leaf-coverage to course down by means of little channels formed in the ground by roots. Without this ministry of many years, the fact is that we could hardly have the gentle farms that many of us know.

Trees, in their own unhurried way – taking many human lifetimes about it – give us cornfields, and steady, dependable water supplies – whether we are grateful for them or not. They save us erosion, in many cases, and the enormous danger to life and limb, of landslides bringing down buildings.

Large areas of steady sands hinder, again and again, the spread of insect pests from one cultivated area to another.

We cannot visualize it, but the mighty Sahara, the experts now tell us, was not always a desert.

Successive generations of nomadic peoples damaged their own livelihood by ignorantly or deliberately clearing their virgin forests. And in some parts of spacious Africa, once thickly populated, this mischief still goes on.

And in mighty America, as I learned, while travelling from publisher to publisher in the course of my work, mischief of another kind is happening to the life of trees. Just printing *one* Sunday edition of a certain metropolitan paper, I'm told, uses up twenty-four acres of forest! An ordinary Chicago daily, I learned when in that city, requires a hundred acres a week! I came away, hoping, in both cases, that my hearing was faulty – but I have seen those giant papers, and my tree-loving heart aches!

I confess that when I am confronted with such a newspaper, or my eye accidentally falls on a trashy sex-thriller, or a trivial magazine, I cannot comfortably forget the words that my poet friend, Teresa Hooley shared with me:

"How many trees have died," she asked,
In all their loveliness and pride —
Home of a myriad wings,
Articulate with wind-taught utterings,
Or tranced in rain-quiet summer eves;
How many trees
For these few worthless leaves?"

★　★　★　★

The time has surely come for all farming people, business magnates and statesmen to study trees –

to fell with discrimination and, where felling must happen, to re-plant.

Too few of us have linked a love of Nature with our Christian Faith, as did Wordsworth, our poet. In a letter he sent to Sir George Beaumont, he rejoiced to write plainly: "I look abroad upon Nature, and I meditate upon the Scriptures, and my creed rises up of itself, with the ease of an exaltation!"

So many about us today, it seems, have not heard that ringing voice of the New Testament, which says: *"Hurt not the earth, nor the trees!"* (Revelation 7:3 – a part of the Bible where we too seldom pause.)

Someone asks: *"What does he do who plants a tree?"* The answer is:

> He plants the friend of sun and sky;
> He plants the flag of breezes free;
> The shaft of beauty towering high;
> For song and mother croon of bird
> In hushed and happy twilight heard.
>
> Anon

To Ponder

> How can one think that trees and flowers
>   and floral scents,
> And plants that grow through sun-drenched
>   hours
> Are accidents?
>
> Behold the dews of dawn's glad hour, or at
>   night's fall,
> The moon, the stars. Is there no Power
>   behind them all?

Oh, call it Nature, if you will;
   you'll not be odd:
I call it someone holier still —
   I call Him "God".

                  Anon

Richard Jefferies, the gifted English naturalist, took to the end of his life, to come to that. Early in his life he scorned any association with revealed religion – the Scriptures and the Church – but toward the end of his days, as he lay listening to his wife reading the Gospel of Luke, he said: "Those are the words of Jesus, and they are true . . . I have done wrong, and thought wrong."

★   ★   ★   ★

O wide-embracing wondrous Love . . .
We read Thee in the flowers, the trees,
The freshness of the fragrant breeze,
The songs of birds upon the wing,
The joy of Summer and of Spring,

But —

We read Thee best in Him who came
To bear for us the Cross of shame,
Sent by the Father from on High,
Our life to live, our death to die.

★   ★   ★   ★

Let Us Give Thanks . . .
Especially for the trees that bring us such delight.

Let us never in any way, grow casual and pass
by such gifts, without true gratitude.

For the changeful immensity of the sky, above the
seasonal beauty below, we bring thanks. And for
all friendships that are strong and good; and hours
unhurried, spent aware of this gift.

For the song of birds, and all simple shapes and
sounds and colours.

Keep us faithful in the caring, keeping ministry
required of us.

For Christ's sake.   AMEN.

R.F.S.

* * * *

Says that choice spirit of our day, Mother Teresa,
"We need to find God, and He cannot be found in
noise and restlessness. God is the Friend of silence;
we see how Nature – trees, flowers, grasses – grows
in silence."

It was a wonder to me – after Mother Teresa
had spoken to a vast company in our city – to share
a few moments alone in talk with her in one of our
tree-blessed parks.

Many of us have our favourite seasons when trees
bless us unforgettably. But they are *all* God's trees,
and God's seasons.

Many amongst us will say with Christina Rosetti
– in spirit, if not in actuality:

Winter is cold-hearted,
  Spring is yes and may,

> Autumn is a weathercock
>   Blown every way:
>   Summer days for me
> When every leaf is on its tree!

More than most men do, Jesus knew trees – He couldn't help but do so as a craftsman in His village, and later whilst moving about His loved countryside on foot.

He had His favourite trees for the rest of His life, one feels sure. He valued many a one, as a place to pray. I felt I knew that for a holy certainty, when, with my dear friend Rene, I was able to spend time in the peacefulness of the trees in Gethsemane.

So Fresh – So Real!

BIBLE CELEBRATION SUNDAY

There are a few mornings, maybe, when one wakens to face the new day "feeling a little flat". Yet I can't think of a reason why any Christian among us need remain that way, "riding on the rims". In the part of the wide world where life set me down, I can, without too much bother, lay hold of the Bible, the most supportive Book in the world, and in my own language. You may have one like it. If, unfortunately for your present mood, it wears a black cover – don't worry. For centuries it has come to fellow-readers that way. But that is no longer necessarily so – your Bible may have a bright blue cover, a lively green, or a challenging red!

A casual reader, browsing at a bookstall set up at an exhibition a while ago, eagerly exclaimed at what she saw there. Taking up a copy of the Bible in its modern binding, she sought out the stallholder, asking: *"Is there anything fresh in it?"*

The answer, of course, is "That depends on its reader – not necessarily on its new cover! *For many of us, there's always something fresh!"* Dr Fosdick spoke of it, as *"The freshest, most joyous Book in the world!"* Those were good words to find a place for in my life, when I was a young Bible student – and I've remembered them ever since!

* * * *

It's a Book full of people — some, in their experience, very like ourselves; others, strangers that we've yet to meet; but all rooted in this one Earth. Many of them are eager to know what comes after. But to many of us the most important issue is what can happen here and now, for this is, above all, a Book centred on *Life's lasting values*. It is a Book full of people — and this is a world full of people! As one American poet says:

> Judas still haggles at his wares,
>   Cain is forever new-created;
> Delilah in a Paris frock,
>   Goes out to tea at five o'clock;
> Potiphar takes the elevated.

Being sophisticated, we all discover in time, does not in itself make life good, unless, as the Bible has long made plain, there are a lot of other "values", too! And the Bible offers us this help in this life, *as no other book does!*

★   ★   ★   ★

Actually, it's not a single book but *a whole library* — whatever its cover! So, it's never the sensible thing to approach it by reading the *first* volume one finds just inside the door then going on through them all, one by one, to the back door — or "cover", as in this unique library volume we call the Bible. Yet surely only a "duffer" would do that? But many "duffers" have actually boasted, within my hearing, of having done that very thing — read the Bible through from cover to cover! (Several have admitted that they got bogged down in Leviticus, or another such book, at the first attempt, but after trying a bit harder, they managed to start again. In time, to their relief, they'd got on from the point at which they'd given up, arriving at the charming little family story of Ruth. After that, somehow, it hadn't seemed such hard going. Then by and by there was the surprising story of Queen Esther; and quite soon that of Job, and his trying experiences; and soon again, "some good parts, in the Psalms, and Proverbs". One old gentleman was very eager to tell me of how he'd come upon the nice parts he liked, "very nice parts!" And I told him of others I liked and had studied: Isaiah; and Nehemiah and his heroic building! But still, it seemed, nobody had ever told him that the Bible was really a library. Said he, "I wish they'd tell us those sort of things in church – and before that, in Sunday School. It's a sort of KEY to the whole thing, isn't it!"

"Yes, to me, it is," I added – and especially to the Old Testament! Some of it history, some song, some biography, travel, family story – and much else. Dr Goodspeed, in his useful book *How To Read The Bible* (Oxford University Press) says:

> The Bible has all the range and variety of a library. It was written on two continents, in three languages, by a hundred authors, scattered over a thousand years. Not only Egypt and Babylon, Palestine and Syria, but Greece and Rome witnessed its origins. Its various parts reflect widely different levels of morals and civilization.

Dr Thielicke, in our own day, speaks of it, and of our reading of it, as "the catching of deep breaths of the air of Eternity".

* * * *

No wonder this precious Book has suffered from the ignorance, and the laziness, of many. It's not to be expected that it will reveal its treasures of life and thought to the casual and careless — and all at once too!

But to those of us who approach it reverently and thoughtfully, and with a little help from a book like that of Dr Goodspeed, or some other which your minister, deaconess, bookseller or best friend can recommend, it will become a life-long companion. Many have spoken of that. "In the Bible," said Coleridge long ago, "there is more that *finds* me than in all the other books put together; the words of the Bible find me at greater depths of my being."

And today — whatever the colour of the cover of one's Bible — to answer the browser at the bookstall, *"There is something fresh in it* here and now, for any one of us who will give a sensible measure of time, and hopeful study, to its rich contents."

* * * *

I must say that in general, the New Testament is *an easier place to start* for a totally new reader — and again, not just inside its cover, with Matthew but with Mark! *Mark is the earliest, the oldest*, part of the New Testament. It's written simply, and eagerly, by a young man who lived in Jerusalem with his mother – one of the earliest Christian home-makers – to whom Jesus, Peter, and the early disciples regularly came. It was, almost certainly, the home where, in its upper guest room, Jesus shared "the Last Supper" with His special friends. (And Peter, the preacher – there that night – was Mark's closest friend, over a long time of coming and going.) From him Mark got a lot to share, that appears nowhere else in any of the other Gospels. (If you haven't come upon it lately, I wrote a little paperback on Mark and his book, as we have it – an exciting introduction to the New Testament. It is called "People and Places" (Fount Paperbacks, Collins). A good starting place for a new Bible reader!)

I have said that the New Testament is an easy place to start. If you want help with the New Testament from end to end, supporting this adventure of yours, after you've learned all you can, it would be a joy to tell you of a shelf of world-famous, pinky-red paperback books I own, published at a very modest price. They are New Testament handbooks written by my late friend, the Scottish scholar, Dr William Barclay.

There is one for each book in the New Testament, and they are easy to read, covering every question that might arise, as you go along. There's an extra one entitled *The Men, The Meaning, The Message of the books*. (It's a long time since I was for years a sales-person in a church bookshop but I can happily tell you of them. You can buy them one at a time, under the overall title *The Daily Study Bible* series. Over five million copies have been sold to this day, according to their publisher. (My friend, in all our talks together, never once mentioned it. He was far too modest. Whilst Professor Barclay was still living, continuing to write and lecture as Professor of Divinity and Biblical Criticism in the University of Glasgow, his publisher wrote of him: "one of the most brilliant Christian expositors of this age." This was not only through his many books, articles and cassette recordings, but also through his frequent appearances on television and radio. (You should have no difficulty in getting these New Testament helps that I am commending so heartily, which should be available from your favourite bookshop, but if you do then concentrate your search on The Saint Andrew Press (121 George Street, Edinburgh), who are the publishers in question. (I add this because it's exasperating to desire such a valuable possession, and yet not know how to lay hold of it.)

We first met in person when I was passing through Glasgow, and William Barclay had already consented to chair a lecture for me. Before we parted that night, he said to me, as a writer friend: "Never come to Glasgow without ringing me up – so that we can sit down to a pot of tea somewhere, *and some good book talk!*" (And I never failed, over the years, as I happily went that way.) In the meantime, I had added others of his books to my "Barclay shelves"; and also dedicated a book of my own to him, *I Believe in the Dawn*, an illustrated hardback then from my English publishers, The Epworth Press: "To my friend, DR WILLIAM BARCLAY, one of the blessed who give without remembering and receive without forgetting."

74

In time, over many years, issue by issue, we each contributed to the same page of a paper then widely read called *The British Weekly*. During that time, I offered to collect and edit some of his articles, for publication as a book that seemed otherwise unlikely to see the light of day. (And a gracious letter came, with his acceptance – "moved," he said, "that in this world, a busy person, as involved as you are, should ever offer to do such a demanding task for another, as busy as I am!"

Through the years, our correspondence on "book-ish things" grew, as my many visits to Britain lessened, by reason of involvement in church matters on my own side of the world.

But "my famous friend" did not forget, and letters continued to find their way to my letterbox, one of them carrying news of his publishing The New Testament in a new two-volume translation that he had "long set his heart on". Time went by, and my thought of it got overlaid. But one day, instead of a neat blue airletter carried by the Postman, there came a sturdy, well-packed parcel: Volume One, "The Gospels and The Acts". And taped inside the handsome volume, a neat note on headed notepaper: "From The Dean of the Faculty of Divinity. The University, Glasgow, W.2." Then my address brought the gift from my long-time encourager:

My dear Miss Snowden,
    Herewith the copy of the translation . . . I send it to you with every good wish and with gratitude

for all that you and your work have meant to me for the last thirty years and more.

> Yours sincerely
> (signed) William Barclay.

(Later, when the second volume came through the press it too was forwarded to complete the set.)

God be praised for all His faithful scholars, writers, and readers!

A Family Celebration

SETTLE ON A TIME

When Francis Wayland Parker, the distinguished educationalist, finished one of his lectures, a woman lost no time in asking her question: "How early," said she, "can I begin the education of my child?"

"When will your child be born?" he asked.

"Born?" she gasped. "Why, he is already five years old!"

"My goodness, woman," he cried, "don't stand there talking to me – hurry home; already you have lost the best five years."

The question from another, was —

> How can we teach
> A child to reach
> Beyond himself and touch the stars,
> We who have stooped so much?
>
> Anon

* * * *

"Children need God," as a wise Christian parent replied to a like question, "not because they are children but because they are people. Childhood is not only preparation for life – it *is* life."

* * * *

With regard to family religion, some have been heard

to say, "The child's mind must be left uninfluenced, until it has arrived at an age when it can choose for itself."

Curiously, we adults do not speak thus of other great issues, such as cleanliness, school rules, table manners, honesty . . .

Coleridge, the poet, was ready with a common-sense answer to a friend who argued in like fashion. "I showed him my garden," said he, "and said it was my botanical garden." "How so?" he answered. "It is covered with weeds." "Oh," replied Coleridge, "that is only because it has not yet come to its age of discretion and choice. The weeds have taken the liberty to grow. I thought it unfair in me to prejudice the soil towards roses and strawberries."

We cannot leave untended the soil of the child-mind. *If we do not plant good and beautiful things, social and moral weeds will be free to grow.*

One little one took her query, *"What is God like?"* to a number of nearby adults:

> I asked my mother what God was like.
>   She did not know.
> I asked my teacher what God was like.
>   She did not know.
> Then I asked my father, who knows more than all
>   Else in the whole world, what God was
>   like.
>   He did not know.
> I think if I had lived as long as
>   My mother and father,
> I would know something about God.

(Could any child you know, say that?)

One of our Master's disciples, Philip, once had a question hardly different. "Lord, show us the Father . . ." Jesus saith unto him:

"Have I been so long time with you,
And yet hast you not known Me, Philip?
He that hath seen Me hath seen the Father!"
John 14:8–9; A.V.

* * * *

It was a great answer, sufficient for Philip, and for countless millions of others of us, ever since! – struggling people, successful people, clever people, puzzled people, young people, middle-aged, or old people!

And it has been proved gloriously so by Jesus Himself, as reported in the Gospels.

Would Christ have prayed *"Our Father"*,
Or cried that name in death,
Unless He first had honoured
Joseph of Nazareth?
    Gilbert Thomas, a poet of our day, puts this
    to us – as we pray.

This great Prayer, "Our Father" (to be found in Matthew 6:9–13; A.V.), never loses its wonder for us, God's Earth children.

One of the very high moments of my life of Christian leadership was when – as Commandant of an English Summer Camp for the Y.W.C.A., held in Sussex, I led ninety girls, speaking in all thirteen different languages, in Family prayers, morning by morning. And each time, over those weeks that we assembled briefly in the beautiful College Chapel, we finished by saying together *The Lord's Prayer*, each in her own tongue. (One couldn't hear the words, but there was a wonderful harmony of Spirit!) I've kept in touch with many of those girls ever since, by letters, and a number of visits to their homes. And our Camp was in 1937 — before the Second World War!

In the long interval since then, a learned guest who shared a pot of tea with me in my home after church, raised a question that for a time stood on the rim of my mind. "It would be good, don't you think," said he, "to give up saying 'The Lord's Prayer', like we do, in church, for a while?" I did not respond by asking him what we should put in its place. There is nothing like it — from childhood through to old age! With some shame, I accepted his unhappy judgement on *the casual way in which we often mutter it*. That's a different thing altogether — and a thousand pities! Only a tiny child should be forgiven for poorly mouthing those glorious words. I'm told that as a very small girl I was overheard praying: "Give us this day *our daily breath.*" (I suppose that wasn't a bad prayer, with all the eager running about we did.)

* * * *

There are many ways in which one can still share

celebrations with children, which don't call for lots of money, but only a loving, caring heart, and a lively imagination. "In days of old, when lights were dim," I found myself once writing, "whole families gathered in the glow of the fire, and told stories. Favourites were told over and over again."

Sometimes storytellers – along with minstrels who strolled through the land singing songs – came and stayed a night or two. It was the only way to hear new stories, because boys and girls then had no books.

But we are more fortunate. Many storytellers today are also writers, and new books are constantly being offered. John Masefield, who wrote of the sea and ships, used to speak of "Children to whom lovely stories are as necessary as pure air". (What I called "daily breath".) And Charles Laughton, the famous actor, also knew this shining truth, and said: "The most beautiful thing in the world to me, is a sea of faces listening to a story."

We need never be lonely. Loved stories can be read or shared over and over, though most children do long for *new* ones – like the little girl whose Bible teacher returned too often to the early passages of Genesis, till the little one could only yawn and say: "I'm tired of the story of the Adamses."

As in books so an element of surprise is essential in all child celebrations – and so it is in those for us grown-up children too!

Someone has sketched in, as nearly as possible, the loss felt by Jesus's Mother, Mary, when she had to see Him grow – and go!

She could not follow where He went,
  She could but watch Him go,
And bless Him, though Her heart was rent
  Because She loved Him so . . .
Distant and dim, heart-sore . . .
  Because She loved Him so!

But of course it wasn't a loss – it was a sharing
of world-wonders for God! A worldwide spiritual
sharing! A life sharing!

A Prayer for All in Our Home
Heavenly Father, as the sun rises, and the day begins,
  bless our home. Let both young and adult give
  thanks for it; and each of us work and play well,
  and happily today.
Bless and help especially all who tend and teach
  little ones; and those who guide and teach eager
  youth.
Let us take care on the busy roads and streets,
  and show patience, and love. For Jesus'
  sake. AMEN.

R.F.S.

A Little Prayer to Say Over
  As each new day comes
    with soft fall of dew,
  God open my eyes
    to serve Thee anew.
R.F.S.

And Another, as I Set Out
 Father of Jesus, my Friend
  and my Father, in Heaven,
 stay close to me where roads bend
  and it's not easy to see.

R.F.S.

A Picnic Prayer
Thank You, God, for winds on high,
 bringing sweetness everywhere,
For green of grass, and blue of sky,
 spelling out Your loving care.

R.F.S.

Gracious God, Giver and Lover of all life, bless our playmates, our pets, and the places where we love to go.

R.F.S.

I have tucked these prayers into this happy book, because prayers are important always – and they don't have to be solemn. But they do have always to be REAL.
So start!
R.F.S.

In the Psalms of the Old Testament is this nice reminder: "GOD SETTETH THE SOLITARY IN FAMILIES" (Psalm 68:6). This is one of the best things He ever did – can you think of others in your daily life?

Lent Strengthens Life

KEEPING THE SEASON OF LENT

Do you agree with my title? Many mistakenly think of Lent as *a lash that pious people apply, for a while, to things they particularly enjoy* – the best seats at the theatre; chocolates in prettily designed boxes; weekends off work for a laze at the beach; a novel just out and bought, without a tedious wait for it from the library. (It may be something like that, even if they do concede that they do not smugly think of it as "proof of the devoted churchgoer that one is".)

But Lent has never been centred on "pride" – far from it! One may reveal a truly religious spirit in the forty weekdays of abstinence, lasting between Ash Wednesday and Holy Saturday, with penance and fasting, harking back to Jesus's own fasting in the Wilderness. And as such it is quietly, faithfully observed by countless Christian people.

St Chrysostom – baptized about the year 376 – was one of the first ever to observe Lent, with its fastings. (So he was a pioneer of a very special kind, as well as a spiritual leader beloved in Constantinople in very early days, when it must have taken a great deal of character to do that.) I had the solitary privilege of moving, bare-footed, about the floor of St Sophia, the mighty building where he centred his ministry, and his Lent-keeping, all that long time ago. Over my head was one of the world's most amazing roofs – and

I moved about, a mere speck below, an experience that I'll never forget.

Famous for his preaching and Lent-keeping, I wondered how anybody ever actually heard him, in that mighty space? (Did "the deaf man" not seat himself in the proverbial "back of the gathering" then as now?)

★ ★ ★ ★

At least, I did happen upon a telling observation he made on Lent-keeping, whilst I moved about St Sophia solitarily, that day. It was:

> Let not the mouth only fast, but also the eye, the ear, the feet, the hands, and all members of the body. Let the hands fast, by learning never to fix themselves on curious or unholy delights. Let the ears fast by not listening to evil speakings and gossip. Let the mouth fast from disgraceful speeches, and all bitterness within.

Is there any more practical "saint" anywhere among us today?

★ ★ ★ ★

As ever at this Season, I turn to that choice, modern book of encouragement that I have on a handy shelf: *Evelyn Underhill's Letters*, written while she was moving amongst friends, offering Christian leadership, in many parts of England. I have read much that she wrote, but never had the pleasure of meeting her in person.

In one letter, to a group of friends, she wrote:

You will remember that in last year's Letter, we considered in some detail the things that we could do to get ourselves into training; reduce comforts and self-indulgence, and perhaps make ourselves more useful to God. Each person's discipline, of course, will be different, because what He wants from each one of us is different. Some are called to an active, and some to a passive life, some to very homely, and some to hard and sacrificial careers, some to quiet suffering. Only the broad lines will be alike. But no discipline will be any use to us unless we keep in mind *the reason why we are doing this — for the Glory of God*, and not for our own self-regarding purpose. Our object is to be what God wants of us, not what we want of Him. *So all that we do must be grounded in worship.*

God expects us each, up through the years, to find our own answers.

One says, simply:

To search our souls,
   To meditate,
Will not suffice
   For Lent.

To share the Cross,
   To sacrifice,
These are the things
   God meant.

Anon

Robert Herrick, one of England's loved early poets (1592–1674), put it like this:

> Is this a Fast to keep
> The larder lean,
> And clean
> From fat of veals and sheep?
>
> No! 'tis a Fast to dole
> The sheaf of wheat
> And meat,
> Unto the hungry soul.
>
> It is to fast from strife,
> From old debate,
> And hate;
> To circumcise thy life.
>
> To show a heart grief-rent;
> To starve thy sin,
> Not bin:
> And that's to keep thy Lent.

My preacher friend, Dr W. E. Sangster, used his telling pulpit prose (later set down in his book *Westminster Sermons*) to say what overflowed from his heart and mind:

> *On every day in Lent* give some time to meditating on the purposes of God on earth, and your relationship to them. You cannot fail to come to Good Friday challenged, humbled . . . and (I trust) redeemed and re-made.

We need this annual "check-up" to our spiritual lives. Even those of us no longer young in
discipleship. I know how easy it is to slip back.
The sheer inertia of our nature, as well as the
unsubdued sin in our souls, tends all the time to
make us drag our feet.

Morning Prayer

O God, I bless Thee that I waken again with a sense
of renewal, to face, as they come, the surprises of
this day – and know Thy supporting Love.

I remember the steady daily work of the village
Carpenter of Nazareth. Let me serve Thee, and
Thy people, with a like spirit, I pray.

Deliver me from the tyranny of trifles, and from
self-concern. Bless, I pray Thee, all beside me,
whose powers of body and mind lessen with age.

Bless all soon coming to retirement, perhaps with
mixed memories. Let their enlarged leisure be a
fulfilling experience – and one to value. Save us,
one by one, this day, from casualness, and total
unconcern for those near us.

Strengthen my spirit, for good living, O Lord of
Life! AMEN.

R.F.S.

Confession and Dedication

Gracious God, my Father, let me be ever mindful
this day that "Guilt is not a state of mind to foster.
True penitence follows on vision of God; guilt is

a barrier between man and God, from which the Gospel offers deliverance. *And Lent is preparation for Easter – the triumph of invincible love and goodness, over all that threatens destruction to personal life."*

From *The Times*, London, in an article from Dr F. R. Barry, former Bishop of Southwell.

Bedtime Prayer, to Add to My Own
Gracious Father, as Thou hast kept me this day so keep me, as night gathers about me, I pray. My daily newspaper does not allow me to forget that this is a violent world. Hold and strengthen, I pray, this night, all whose work in the community is concerned with crime. Keep them – and their families – true and faithful.   AMEN.

R.F.S.

Morning Prayer
Ever-Forgiving Lord of Life, quicken our awareness of Thy nearness, especially if there is anything new ahead today – anything of which we are unsure, even a little afraid.
And let *me* not think only of my own concerns – let me say something, or do something, this day, that will make a welcome difference to someone.
Give me clear eyes to see things in proper perspective – and wisdom to handle them in a good spirit – in the Name of Christ.   Amen.

R.F.S.

Christmas – and Always

Daily Reading of a Psalm

It is good to give thanks to the Lord,
   To sing praises to Thy name, O Most High.
To declare Thy steadfast love in the morning,
   And Thy faithfulness by night . . .
For Thou, O Lord, hast made me
   glad by Thy work;
At the works of Thy hands I sing for joy!

Psalm 92: 1.4; R.S.V.

Evening Prayer

Father, I bless Thee for this day's end,
   when the weary can rest.
Our Master, many a time on earth, knew
   such a good gift.
Often, He sought peace in the hills – and
   time to pray.
Once, at least, He fell asleep in Peter's
   little boat.
For this day's end of busyness, I bless Thee
   now.   AMEN.

R.F.S.

Paul Wrote to His Friends in Thessalonica

These words have become precious to many others:

God has not destined us for wrath, but to obtain
salvation through our Lord Jesus Christ, Who died
for us so that *whether we wake or sleep* we might live
with Him.

1 Thessalonians 5:9; R.S.V.

Unforgettable

MAUNDY CELEBRATION

The colours of the day were encouraging. I was in London, alone, and going to the Maundy Service in Westminster Abbey.

The Abbey was filling – indeed, it was already almost full, as I had been told it would be, when, a day or two earlier, I made enquiries about a seat. I found myself part of a hushed, reverent company, seated well toward the front.

Soon, we all rose to the strains of the processional hymn, "Praise my soul . . .", with shafts of sunlight coming down to us from the tall windows. Our King, George VI, gracing the Service with his presence, was, as most of us by this time knew, already a frail man – and we were glad that he was present, honouring the importance of the Service.

It was a beautiful Service and very simple – as was fitting. The beadle, bearing the mace, entered – then came the slow majestic procession through to the Choir. In their respective places came the children of the Royal Almonry, the Abbey choristers, the almoners, and the royal bodyguard of Yeoman of the Guard, adding colour to the scene with their Tudor scarlet and gold.

The derivation of the word "Maundy" is, of course, meant to commemorate Jesus's humble washing of the disciples' feet (John 13:1–17; A.V.).

A little obscure now, as a word that has dropped out of usage, concerning the "command" of the Master, on that occasion long ago. At one time, foot-washing was actually carried out in the Abbey Service, but Queen Elizabeth I was, it seems, the last to do that. These days, the Service is simplified, and royal gifts of little purses holding a few specially-minted coins are substituted. These are much valued by these elderly folk entitled to receive them on each occasion – as many men and women as there are years in the Sovereign's age at the time. The little purses holding the coins, of red leather with white thongs, and white leather with red thongs, are carried into the Service on a great silver-gilt dish. (This, as it happened, was placed on a table close to where I sat, at the foot of the Sanctuary steps.)

As part of the Service came Prayers in which we joined; and Lessons, (appropriately John 13, and Matthew 25 – with its message, in verse 40: "*Inasmuch . . .*") Then came a Psalm, and two Anthems.

Twice during the Service the King left his seat, and came down among the poor people who had come from many parts of the country to receive the royal gifts, at his hand.

At the conclusion of the two distributions came the General Thanksgiving, in accordance with ancient custom, "the priest and people kneeling". And so, with brief prayers, the singing of the Old Hundredth, the Blessing, and the National Anthem, the Service came to an end. So simple, so colourful, and right, that peace fell upon our spirits.

Rather than come out by the way I had entered, I returned through the aisle with many others, where I noticed an old gentleman, holding his Maundy money. I stopped to talk to him. He was snowy-headed, and bent. "This is a great day for you," I said as we shook hands there. "Yes," said he, "and many's the time I never thought to see it."

"Well, I am glad that you do see it," said I. "And I'm glad that I see it myself. I've come a long way – right round the world, from New Zealand."

"I been there," said he, to my surprise. "I been to Wellington, I been to Auckland."

"Surely," I said, "that was a long time ago."

"Yes. I was an officer in a sailing vessel in them days," he answered me. "And I got wrecked in the Bristol Channel, ma'am, with eighty tons of gelignite aboard. And there was times when I never thought to see this day." Then he paused, but only to say a lovely thing: "I seen sights all round the world: but I never seen nothing better than this – *the King, a humble serving man!*"

★ ★ ★ ★

I was several years too late to tell that experience to my dear home-keeping Mother – she would have loved it. But I'm not too late to re-tell a story of *her*, bearing the same humble spirit. And I believe you will love it, just as truly.

When last I was able to go back on a brief visit to the setting of our old home, both my Father and my Mother had "gone upon their way". Some, who were as good homemakers as she was, in their day – but can't do much now – spoke of her. They spoke very warmly, and in the one breath, of her Sunday school, and her apron. I suppose it was not odd really, but only the most natural thing. I hardly remember her at home without a cleanly fresh apron. It has its place in the last sight at the gate as I left home for the first time, in young adulthood, to go to my studies. And in the first glimpse I caught of her as she welcomed me back at the end of term; and when, with but half-an-hour's warning, she left us at the close of one day we shall always remember, *she was wearing her apron.*

One day, later on, working away at a piece of writing as I was already doing, I had occasion to open an old dictionary, and allow Mr Webster to tell me what an apron is. *"An apron,"* said he, *"is a portion of cloth . . . worn as a protective covering in front of one's person."* But I have the feeling that the good man knew very little about it. A verse in Peter's writing in the Moffatt New Testament (1 Peter 5:5) is much nearer the point. He says: "You must all put on *the apron of humility to serve one another."* My mother did just that. She kept her home. Her tins were always full of cookies; she gave away bottles of milk to her Sunday school children who came from large families; jars from her precious preserve cupboard, and, as a special treat, delicious blackcurrant jam in winter-time. In summer, it would be something else – fruit from our family trees, baskets filled with plums, ripe gooseberries, a dozen other joys of a child's palate; *and always, with a cleanly fresh apron on!*

She didn't wear it to church – or, at least, I don't remember that she did, even by mistake, under her coat on a winter's night. But *she wore the spirit* of it there, as she wore it everywhere. And Dr Moffatt's lovely rendering of Peter's words still lingers along with thoughts of my mother: *"You must all put on the apron of humility to serve one another!"* 1 Peter 5:5

★　★　★　★

She grew fond of those Sunday school children, and earned their love by offering her own. It was one of those simple things that happen in country places. Interest grew – it was bound to grow – and numbers grew. Her big class of boys surrounded her with love, and a sort of comradeship, long after they were coming along in their first long pants! And birthdays and Christmases brought to her door, year by year, something nice they'd seen in the village store window – a new dish, perhaps, that she would have bought for a mother of any one of them, for Christmas, or Birthday.

To Ponder

Acts of humility – to remain gracious and serviceable – call first for a humble heart, a right spirit.

No wonder Cardinal Wolsey failed to keep a true Maundy Thursday at Peterborough Abbey in 1530, though he washed and kissed the feet of fifty-nine poor men. And after wiping them, gave to each man twelve pence in cash, three ells

of good canvas to make them a shirt, a pair of new shoes, three white herrings, and three red herrings!
But things, alone, do not count!

R.F.S.

In our modern times, T. S. Eliot, the poet, felt he had to say

The only wisdom we can hope to acquire
Is the wisdom of humility: humility is endless.

It didn't happen most truly, first in a Holy Book.
It happened in a hospitable upper room, among friends!

R.F.S.

* * * *

Our Lord and Master is still concerned with our daily ploys, as well as with our prayers, offered quietly, head bowed, in the family pew, and draws no line between our services offered for His Kingdom, in terms of "sacred" and "secular".

R.F.S.

* * * *

Prayer For Today
Eternal God, revealed in Christ our Saviour and
    Lord, I rejoice in Thy power and purpose in the
    familiar tasks facing me today.
Thou hast set me to serve Thy Kingdom, in this
    place, and time. Let the sacredness of human life,
    and service, come home to me anew.
I bless Thee that I am allowed to know Thy love

and keeping. And in so many ways to lay hold of Thy strength, in my human needs.

I praise Thee for the rising sun, and the seasons – and all the surprises they bring. With every new day, grant me a ready awareness, and a new eagerness for life.

In the Name of Christ, my Master.   AMEN.

R.F.S.

* * * *

A Silent Prayer as I Serve

O Master, ever near, bless my Service today – the planned part of it – and the unexpected. And help me to be outreaching to the people about me.

Give me courage, O Lord, to attend to those things I ought to this day. Deliver me from the temptation to put them off till another time.   AMEN.

R.F.S.

* * * *

A Workday Prayer from Wesley's Brother

Son of the Carpenter, receive this humble work of mine;

Worth to my meanest labour give, by joining it to Thine!

Charles Wesley

* * * *

A Prayer for Any Hour or Place

Gracious God, I rejoice that I am allowed to live in Thy great world! Greater than Thy majesty is Thy love; more lasting than all is Thy mercy. Hold me, loyal and caring, in all the comings and goings of this day, I ask Thee – in the Name of Christ, Thy Son.   AMEN.

R.F.S.

★   ★   ★   ★

A Prayer for Here and Now
O Lord, let no selfish passion, no stupidity of mine, no lowered standard of behaviour make life harder for anyone about me. Give me gladness, clear vision, and a kind tongue. Deliver me from all insincerity. For Christ's sake.   AMEN.

R.F.S.

There Is No Legacy Like It

CELEBRATING PEACE

Rain had fallen heavily in the last few days. Most of us had been soaked, getting about on foot. But this morning brought shafts of sunlight into my little kitchen.

Breakfast over, I put my city-going bag and documents together. I had been poring over the revision of my Will, and now had a clear copy to carry from my typewriter, into the hard-headed business city. I had arranged to travel by the earliest bus, which would be pleasant on such a morning – and good to get this bit of business off my mind.

★ ★ ★ ★

A few office-going folk were already at the nearest bus stop, chatting about the damage done by the recent storm. Lots of tree branches had been bashed down, and from our high seats, as we travelled, we caught sight of many more on the far side of low hedges.

But in no time, it seemed, I was surging along with another throng on our city's busiest streets, to the entry of a large block of buildings, and then in a lift to my lawyer's office. We'd not seen each other for some time, so we exchanged greetings, and asked after family health. But soon, our joint thoughts were of the drawing up of Wills, and the revision of mine.

Comfortably seated, we displayed our documents on the spacious desk, already cleared for the purpose.

★   ★   ★   ★

"I've often had to notice," said old David Harum – long, long before either of us was born – "that a man'll sometimes do the foolishest thing, or the meanest thing in his whole life, after he's dead." True! And many a one, I found myself reflecting as I sat there, had been grieved, if not angered. A pity – when for so long, plans have been available to prevent such a thing happening. So much, it seemed, depended on a person's *good heart*. There is now no reason for a Will resulting in a miserly act.

One person without mention of a lawyer to render him legal help, was Shakespeare. Being a man of the pen, likely he felt able to manage on his own. The surprising thing was that he had so little to leave – a modest provision for members of his family, and remembrances to several friends; but to his wife, he willed only "his *second-best bed, and furniture*".

I had gained insight into these meaningful matters from Reginald Hine's delightful tome *The Confessions of an Un-Common Attorney*, which stood on my own bookshelves. Though I seldom take it down for a browse in these busy days, there are passages in it that I know almost off by heart. And when I got the chance, I paid a visit to his old town of Hitchin, with all its charms. Reginald Hine had only a little while before "gone upon his way"; but there were still many about who had known him well. A friend of mine had married a gentleman of Hitchin.

Hine had been apprenticed as a youth to one of the oldest legal firms in all England, with prized access to documents going back into the sixteen hundreds. Little wonder he had so much to share about early Wills!

"To an old-fashioned person like myself," he wrote, "there is so much to miss, and deplore in the form and subject matter of modern testaments. One felt happier, legally and religiously, about Wills that opened with the hallowed invocation: 'In the name of God. Amen.' Nor was His name taken in vain when the testator went on to 'bequeath my soule to Almighty God, and to all the holy company of hevyn.' "

In the course of time, the form had to be modified to suit the religious innovations of the age. By the end of the fifteenth century, and into the sixteenth, "oure blissed Saint Mary the Virgyne his glorious modre" was joined as legatee. After the Reformation, "the holy company of hevyn" and "our blissed lady" were cut out; testators put their trust instead in "the death and passion of Jesus Christe", or threw themselves upon the mercy of "the Comforter". (So that up to the seventeenth century, at any rate, the making of a Will was something of a holy task, whatever it has become now.) "But what can one do in this religiously slack age?" asks many a one of us, as well as "the Un-common Attorney", with people who are doubtful whether they possess a soul to be bequeathed or saved?

The presence of modern uncertainty can be seen in the Will of Margaret Albury, as early as 1800.

"My books," she begged, "to be divided amongst the family, as they can agree. But I hope there will be no words. Pray don't sell none of my books." Poor Margaret! The sharing of her treasures, at the end of the day, is all too plainly fraught with uncertainties.

A good time earlier, one Gerald had left "To Mary my daughter twenty pounds; the featherbed that I lye upon, the bolsters and coverlets of tapestrye work, with a blanket, four payres of shetts that is to say four payres of the best flaxen, and other two payres of the best hempen, the greate brasse potte that was hir mothers, the chaffing dish that hangeth in the parlor." *There* seems a steady confidence – but was Mary the only benefactor?

Looking across the years, to the Will of May Swain, spinster of Preston hamlet (1784), it seems that she had no family to love, or quarrel with – and little to leave. "To my niece Mary Swain", her Will reads, "my best stays and my worst, together with the nut-meg-grater and the jack-and-spit. To Mary Doggett my second-best stays, my red cloake and a frying-pan." (There is unlikely to be an entry in your Will, or mine, in this day and age, to approach that!)

Richard Phearndeane, a labourer in Sussex, in the same spirit, left to his brother Stephen what little he had: "My white dublett, best jerkin and best shoes", and to Bernard Rogge, "my white dublett and worst breeches". (Compared with these, my list – laboured over lately at home, and at the right moment, placed on my lawyer's desk – seemed "colourless".)

But then, the test of a legacy, *is not only in*

material things! The best of materials tarnish; and "moth and dust doth corrupt!" This was why the loved preacher, scholar, and writer of books on my shelves, Dr A. J. Gossip, delighted in the phrase, *The Legacy of Christ.* Our Lord had all too few material things of value, unless we count His cloak "woven without seam", a lovely thing – but the soldiers on duty at His cross took that, as their dues.

His "legacy" was, in actuality, a yet lovelier thing. Speaking to His closest friends, He said: *"My Peace* I give unto you!" (John 14:27; A.V.).

"Not as the world giveth, give I unto you. Let not your heart be troubled, neither let it be afraid!" Another long-time friend, the noted Scottish preacher and scholar, Dr J. S. Stewart, called that *"The Last Will and Testament of Jesus".* It was not a Will written upon a piece of perishable parchment – He wrote on nothing of that kind, but only on the ground, in the dust at His sandalled feet, to support a poor, unfortunate woman hauled before Him in a merciless moment.

His friends were to possess His Peace – as a gift, in mercy given! And it is still so – as you and I have lived to discover. *And a glorious legacy it is!* I can say no more – whether speaking to a company; or writing to one person alone – and neither could Paul, in his changeful, crowded life, as recorded confidently in Romans 10:11; Moffatt's Translation: *"No one who believes in Him, will ever be disappointed. No one!"*

Dr William Barclay, soaked in the meaning of New Testament words, and matching them with real life experience, was always reminding us that the

Greek word for Peace occurs in the New Testament eighty-eight times, so there is no way that we could regard it as accidental. As our title proclaims: *"There is no legacy like it!"*

* * * *

A Thought to Live With
In another part of the New Testament (Philippians 4:7), Paul writes of this life gift, as "The Peace of God which passeth all understanding".

Says Dr W. R. Maltby, "ordinary people, if they want religion at all, want it to live by – not merely to think about."

* * * *

Peace is Precious
J. Ramsay Macdonald, early in his busy life in politics, and pushed hither and thither, wrote of his young wife Margaret's discovery: "She had within her being a Holy of Holies . . . Late autumn and winter, with the moan of the sea passing over the land like the cry of toiling creation . . . she would retire within herself and go out silently to the shore, or the moors, in quest of something which haunts like a dim vision of a strange beauty, or a confused echo of a far away melody."

* * * *

A Morning Prayer
Gracious God, I rejoice in this day's new light; in
  the feeling of well-being that leads me to thanks;
  And to look towards familiar opportunities for

service.

I bless Thee for friends, who for long years have crossed over my doorstep – enriching my life in so many rewarding ways.

In these days, I am one of many living alone in maturity; yet in the most real sense *wrapped round in Your Peace*. Now, as ever.   AMEN.

Anon

★　★　★　★

A Little Poem to Ponder
  Prince of Peace —
    This is the miracle I seek,
      O Living Christ,
    Your strength and purpose in my hands,
    Your kindness in my voice,
    Within my heart Your certainty of God,
    Your love for all mankind.
    Dr George MacLeod speaks of it, as "the so-called spiritual, and the so-called material."

Christ always made it plain, that Peace could be a real possession!

★　★　★　★

An Evening Prayer
O Lord God, from time to time, others, tired as I am, have turned aside to remember at day's end, Whose they are, and Whom they serve, and to give thanks. And I do that now.

Remembering —— and —— and their needs, as well as my own, at this day's end. And to seek for them, too, Thy safe keeping through the night. Let the pattern of their relaxation be one of Christ's Peace. For His dear sake.   AMEN.

R.F.S.

But a Donkey Can Do It

PALM SUNDAY "The Sunday Before Easter"
Isn't it surprising what people will collect? Old
silver spoons, luggage labels, coloured scarves, etc.,
etc.

But then, I collect *opening sentences*! The best one
I ever came upon was in Westminster Central Hall,
London. It was sermon time, and a long-time friend,
Dr Will Sangster, was in the pulpit, and before him a
fine congregation. Eyebrows went up, I confess, as
he broke the silence with: "There is nothing dignified
about a donkey."

It was Palm Sunday, and with our rapt attention,
the preacher went on. Christ, with the uncertain
company of crowded streets, was making His way
into Jerusalem – *seated on a donkey!* Mostly he walked
about the world by meadow paths – but this was
different. There was no room to move easily, and
the crowd was in an unaccountable mood! It was
dangerous, and He knew it would be!

But He had planned His movements well ahead,
as is clear in John's Gospel (11:55–57, and 12:12 on;
Good News Bible).

The time for the Passover Festival was near, and
many people had come up from the country to
Jerusalem . . . they were looking for Jesus, and
as they gathered in the Temple, they asked one
another, "What do you think? Surely He will not

107

come to the festival, will He?" The chief priests and the Pharisees had given orders that if anyone knew where Jesus was, he must report it, so that they could arrest Him.

Six days before the Passover, Jesus went to Bethany, the home of Lazarus, the man He had raised from death. They prepared a dinner for Him there, which Martha helped to serve; Lazarus was one of those who were sitting at the table with Jesus . . . A large number of people heard that Jesus was in Bethany, and they went there . . . So the chief priests made plans to kill Lazarus too, because on his account many Jews were rejecting them and believing in Jesus.

The next day the large crowd that had come to the Passover Festival heard that Jesus was coming to Jerusalem. So they took branches of palm trees and went out to meet Him, shouting, "Praise God! God bless Him who comes in the name of the Lord! God bless the King of Israel!"

Jesus found a donkey and rode on it, just as the Scripture says,

Do not be afraid, city of Zion,
Here comes your King,
riding on a young donkey.

His disciples did not understand this at the time; but when Jesus had been raised to glory, they remembered that the Scripture said this about Him and that they had done this for Him.

"The humble donkey", I learn from authorities, "was not introduced into England before the first

Queen Elizabeth's time – and seemed a stranger when spoken of, in the New Testament sense, as carrying our Lord into Jerusalem." But today, Christians rejoice in this humble service – and the reply it was arranged the two disciples should give, when earlier they untied the waiting animal at an agreed spot (Mark 11:1–7; A.V.) "If any man say unto you, 'Why do ye this?' Say ye, that *the Lord hath need of him.*" (And all down the centuries since, that has been the one adequate answer concerning the doer of many a humble deed in Christ's service: *"The Lord hath need of him"* – and that is enough!

In the same mood, they like to point out that today "a dark stripe runs along the back of such a donkey, and another crosses it over the shoulder", as the learned *Encyclopaedia Britannica* records. It seems now highly fitting that such lowly service long ago should be marked *with a cross*!

That comes to my mind, beautifully, tellingly, every time I go back to the glorious Cathedral of Winchester in England. William Walker was "the donkey" of Christ, on one unforgettable occasion, there, when the Lord "had need of him".

The ancient building was sinking; parts had already sunk two feet, arches had become distorted, cracks were visible. Eight feet down the masonry was found to stop; the medieval building had been set on a raft of logs above a reclaimed bog. Now, it was decided to send down a diver to see what was happening, and William Walker was that man.

Grovelling in black ooze, no light penetrating, he brought up peat, a handful at a time. In its place, with water pumped out, he laid bags of cement, till with his hands he settled a new foundation. *So the glorious building stands today!*

And each day, as it breaks for us, waits for what *our* humble hands can do. Even in these modern times "the Lord hath need of them". In that spirit, I set down here T. Hornblower Gill's words for us to memorize:

> Darkness and dread we leave behind;
> New light, new glory still we find,
> New realms divine possess . . .
> We stay at home, we go in quest,
> Still Thou art our abode.
> The rapture swells, the wonder grows,
> As full on us new life still flows
> From our unchanging God.

* * * *

My Constant Prayer

It is wonderful, O God, to waken again refreshed, possessed of all my faculties.

It is wonderful to have people and things to get up for, and to serve all this day.

Let the sacredness of home life and human relationships outside come strongly through all I plan and do this day.

Let the wonder of human achievement be lightened by devotion to Your good purposes in the world, here and afar.

Let those who devote their energies to peacemaking among the nations know Your righteous strength and encouragement today.

Let those who till the soil and plant and harvest be good stewards of your earth entrusted to them, and make them ready to share with the needy.

Let those gifted above their fellows use their powers this day for the upholding of all things good and honest and true, and not for smashing down.

Let all who labour to lighten the lot of others, especially —— and —— among the many I know, have Your blessing this day. For Christ's sake. Amen.

From my own *A Woman's Book of Prayers*.

* * * *

Evening Prayer

The day is done, O God, and I hush my heart again for a few moments.

Forgive me, if I have wavered in my Christian witness when I have been with others;

If I have hesitated at the crossroads of choice, when the way needed courage;

If I have dreamed of great things, and failed in the little ones;

If I have gone about things solemnly, forgetting fun and laughter;

If I have allowed myself to be so busy, that no one dare tell me her troubles;

If I have shown impatience with anyone doing his best.

Bless this night any I know who do not pray for themselves;

Any I know separated from those they love especially

—— and ——

And any still living together, whose hearts have
 drifted apart;

Any who have done things today that now fill
 them with shame;

Any who have suffered an accident, or in some
 other way found this a specially difficult day,

Be so real to us each that we may lie down in
 Your peace.   AMEN.

A Woman's Book of Prayers.

*   *   *   *

Dr W. E. Sangster said, very tellingly, in that same
Palm Sunday sermon I heard him preach, and from
which I collected his "opening sentence":

> *He has been using ordinary men ever since, and doing*
> *mighty things with them. He doesn't work only with*
> *the geniuses.* He will work with anybody who will
> give Him a consecrated heart. He is displeased with
> those who shrink away from His call, cuddling
> their inferiorities and saying: "I'm not clever, or
> saintly, or ten-talented. I can't do anything." The
> Christ Who made use of a despised animal could
> make greater use of you, and, if He doesn't, it will
> be because you won't let Him.

*   *   *   *

G. K. Chesterton, the beloved, in his day was not
ashamed to identify himself with the donkey. Said
he – and in words that have never been forgotten:

The tatter'd outlaw of the earth,
   Of ancient crooked will;
Starve, scourge, deride me, I am dumb,
   I keep my secret still.

Fools! For I also had my hour,
   One far fierce hour and sweet;
There was a shout about my ears,
   And palms about my feet!

            ★   ★   ★   ★

Morning Prayers
Bless all who worship Thee, from the rising of the
   sun unto the going down of the same. Of Thy
   goodness, give us; With Thy love, inspire us; by
   Thy Spirit, guide us; by Thy power, protect us;
   in Thy mercy, *receive us now and always.* Amen.
            From *Divine Worship* – approved for
            optional use in Methodist Churches

John Burton's sung petition never dated, nor did
its dedication —

Send me, Lord, where Thou wilt send me,
   Only do Thou guide my way;
May Thy grace through life attend me,
   Gladly then shall I obey.

Let me do Thy will, or bear it;
   I would know no will but Thine:
Shouldst Thou take my life or spare it,
   I that life to Thee resign.

How Good Is Good Friday?

JESUS CARRIES THE CROSS

I can't recall the occasion when I first sought an answer to the question I have set at the top of our page today, but never to be forgotten is one morning when, alone, I visited St Alban's Abbey. It was early on an ordinary weekday, and at that hour few others were about. Tourists who had learned what was quietly happening at Verulamium, the one-time proud Roman city, were not yet stirring. It was hard to visualize that, beneath the pleasant grassy area where I stood, busy workmen had for some time been on the spot with their shovels, and some extraordinary finds had come to light – an old piece of Roman wall, a mosaic floor of rare beauty, a hypocaust (an underground heating system), a theatre.

But the quiet workman with whom I talked, had beside him something that interested me more – a small bucket of Roman coins that had not been handled for many a day; and, what was to me even more interesting, another small bucket of twisted, hand-made Roman nails. When he saw my reaction he added: "These would have been like those used on Good Friday! See – about four inches long; hammered, with square heads. All twisted, and rusted now – but cruel!" And with those words, he stooped silently, and picked out three, and placed them in my hand. When I received them without a word, he simply said: "Perhaps you'd like them – there are, as you see for the record, plenty here." And he returned several very twisted ones to the bucket.

It was, for me, a moment never to be forgotten. As a traveller, I never carry home "mementos", trifles from tiny tourist shops, in places I find myself visiting. *But these were different!*

And from Good Friday to Good Friday, they lodge in a secret place I have, dear to my heart, only being taken out when I am asked to address a church gathering on Good Friday! They have a unique power, it seems, of reminding us of the utter down-to-earth reality of the Scripture I read!

★　★　★　★

All too easily, with the years, we grow accustomed to the Authorized Version, for all the beauty of its diction – having read it countless times – so it's a good thing, on an important occasion, to make use of another version, as I have this time, in turning to the "Good News Bible", with which I am less familiar. In John 19:16 it is written:

> Then Pilate handed Jesus over to them to be crucified. So they took charge of Jesus. He went out carrying his cross, and came to "The Place of the Skull", as it is called. (In Hebrew it is called "Golgotha".) There they crucified Him; and they also crucified two other men, one on each side, with Jesus between them. Pilate wrote a notice and had it put on the cross: "Jesus of Nazareth, the King of the Jews" . . . Many people read it.

Now read on in the version you choose.

* * * *

Night Prayer

O God, the darkness of this hour we hold in sorrow, seems darker as we recall the cruelty of many on that occasion.

And sadder, as we think back to the presence of Mary, Mother of the Crucified.

But it holds something precious at the heart of my Faith in the wholeness of Christ's Sacrifice — for evermore.

I marvel at the loving concern Jesus showed for the two suffering at His side. And for Disciple John, His faithful friend. And the little knot of suffering, faithful women.

At this point of Time, our human comprehension is at a loss to spell out the measure of Redeeming Love. But we know — through Faith — it leads on to a Greater Revelation!   AMEN.

R.F.S.

* * * *

A Later Prayer

Gracious Redeemer, we pause to give thanks for Thy Dying Love!

That Joseph of Arimathea was moved to offer his own tomb, as a token of dignity, amid the cruelty of Death.

For the good caring of the women present, who hastened home to prepare sweet burial spices, we bless Thee.

Let us find a way to show our Love, we
pray. Amen.

R.F.S.

* * * *

From "A Manual For Ministers"
Grant, O Lord of Righteousness, that as we gaze
upon our Lord on whom was laid the burden of
men's transgressions, we may be moved with true
penitence, lest in our own day we crucify afresh the
Lord of life and King of love. Amen.

* * * *

A hymn, long and widely beloved
When I survey the wondrous Cross
On which the Prince of Glory died,
My richest gain I count but loss,
And pour contempt on all my pride.

See, from His head, His hands, His feet,
Sorrow and love flow mingled down;
Did e'er such love and sorrow meet,
Or thorns compose so rich a crown?

Were the whole realm of nature mine,
That were an offering far too small;
Love so amazing, so divine,
Demands my soul, my life, my all.

Isaac Watts

* * * *

And sitting down, they watched Him there,

The soldiers did;
There, while they played with dice,
He made His sacrifice,
And died upon the Cross to rid
God's world of sin.

And ere his agony was done,
Before the westering sun went down,
Crowning that day with its crimson crown,
He knew that He had won.

                              G. A. Studdert-Kennedy

* * * *

Thanksgiving

I heard two soldiers talking
As they came down the hill —
The sombre hill of Calvary;
Bleak and black and still.
One said, "The night is late;
These thieves take long to die."
And one said, "I am sore afraid,
And yet I know not why."

I heard two women weeping
As down the hill they came,
And one was like a broken rose,
And one was like a flame.
One said, "Men shall rue
This deed their hands have done."
And one said only through her tears,
"My Son! My Son! My Son!"

                              Anon

★　★　★　★

But some words of Dr Stanley Jones, of our day, are also not to be forgotten:

Life's last word is not a Cross . . . What is man's slander if God affirms? What is Calvary, if just beyond it lies an *Easter Morning*?

Rejoice with those who do rejoice – your Lord God reigneth!

★　★　★　★

Few of us, I think, will know Peter Abelard's (1079–1142) verse from his "Hymn for Good Friday", but it is full of Faith.

This is that night of tears, the three days' space,
　　Sorrow abiding of the eventide,
Until the day break with the risen Christ,
　　And hearts that sorrowed shall be satisfied.

"Christian Faith is essentially Faith in the Resurrection. Faith in the Resurrection means being born again to Hope. The risen Christ makes life a continual *Festival*, a *Festival without end*," said Athanasius. And we, of this modern day, delight to echo it, with all our hearts!

R.F.S.

★　★　★　★

Our Morning Prayer is

Gracious God, Father of our everlasting spirits, our

thoughts just now are of the injustice, loneliness, and deadly hurt attending Christ, our Lord and Saviour, on this world's first "Good Friday".

Thoughts of His anguish, and utter Self-giving, only become ours from what the early New Testament records have so tellingly shared. So that the last word is not "Hurt", but "Love" and "Forgiveness" beyond all human imagining.

But Your Divine ways are always so much above our poor human ways, that we are left to accept them with lasting Wonder and Praise. And this we do, here and now, as ever, on *this* Good Friday morning.   AMEN.

R.F.S.

★   ★   ★   ★

Our Night Prayer is

We thank Thee, Lord, that Thou hast brought us through this day, remembering sad realities.

We marvel at the loving-care that Christ showed for the two suffering alongside Him! At the faithful followers – from near and far – especially the women folk, and His gentle Mother, Mary, and His disciple, John, the beloved.

We bless Thee, too, for him who lent the Crucified his own new tomb, wherein no man had yet lain, to provide some human dignity at Death!

★   ★   ★   ★

And we bless thee, that a woman, Mary, the faithful, came to meet Him alive – risen from that

very Tomb! Enable us each – as long as life lasts
– to be as faithful, for His Dear Sake.   AMEN.
R.F.S.

A Moment of Amazement

EASTER

As a visitor from the far parts of the world, I was not in the least prepared for what awaited me in Cambridge. I arrived in the gentle evening, but it was too late for my colour camera, so I picked out a pleasing position, from the edge of the green sward and beneath a break in the trees, offering me the beautiful buildings beyond. I would be back in the morning, I told myself.

But to my amazement, by mid-morning, there was no green sward – a miracle had occurred! It was a spring miracle, for where last night I had visualized myself standing, there was now *a blaze of newly-risen crocuses!*

It was Easter – with its glorious message of Life! And as I made my way to worship, John Krumm's words came alive for me: *"Easter is God's way of looking at Good Friday!"* From earliest Christian times, this celebration, I told myself, had been joyously important, and it had remained lastingly important, spelling out LIFE in the place of human hurt, suffering and death! It mattered not that early Christians had long celebrated the Resurrection of their Lord without giving that glorious season a name. It was a surprise to find the name in the New Testament – but there it is an anachronism, as it appears (in Acts 12:4; A.V.) to suggest a time of year with its parallel Feast. (We have, most of us, likely never even noticed the verse.) It refers to Herod *"intending after Easter"* to do such-and-such a thing. But it won't be wasted, if it serves as a check to us of what *we* intend to do after Easter, having celebrated the Resurrection of our Lord, and all that it means; what "The New Testament in Basic English" calls *"death and coming back from death"*.

But with greater, joyous confidence we can lay hold of Paul's words: *"If Christ be not risen, then is our preaching vain, and your Faith is also vain."* (1 Corinthians 15:14; A.V.).

★ ★ ★ ★

But our Faith, this Eastertide, and every Easter, is —

Our wayside planet, carrying land and wave,
Love and life multiplied, and pain and bliss,
Bears as chief treasure one forsaken grave.
Alice Meynell

★ ★ ★ ★

"Among the many other things that Easter means to the Christian," says Richard Harries, formerly Dean of King's College, London, in his little Fount Paperback *Prayer and the Pursuit of Happiness*, it must also mean a particular sense of proportion about our griefs and sufferings. They hurt, sometimes excruciatingly, but, on the deepest level of all, it is somehow "all right", and, out of the praise and gratitude and joy that spring from it, when we can grasp it, I think we can give ourselves permission for the more mundane, but wonderfully healing emotion of happiness."

And Richard Harries adds, only a few pages on, lest we should miss something precious: *"The Joy of Christ is the Joy of His Resurrection, and continuing Presence with us."* This is a Joy which no one can take away from us; for nothing, not even death, can separate us from Christ's Love for us."

* * * *

A Presbyterian friend, the Rev. Peter Beer, lived at the other end of my town; though happily not too far away. Not much time went by without our sharing plans, and themes, over a cup of tea. I was writing books, no longer broadcasting; but he was still doing that occasionally, as part of an exceedingly busy ministry.

The Easter Celebration came, and brought him to the "mike", with a brief, telling message "that just needed," said he, "a brief witness" from me. What I had taken from my heart, but an hour or so before, was still lying with other work on my desk. I copied it out for him, and during Easter Day's Worship, *heard it over the air*:

* * * *

Hang out your Hallelujahs!
the Tomb is open,
the Roman guard gone,
Death defeated!
The Man of Life walks again,
comforting the troubled,

healing the sick,
forgiving sinners!
                    R.F.S.

★   ★   ★   ★

Vital, Easter experiences of the spirit never date.
What Francis Kilvert wrote in his time (between
1840 and 1879) could have been as tellingly shared
with you and me, on the Easter closest to us in time.
He wrote describing it as

> the happiest, brightest, most beautiful Easter I
> have ever spent. I woke early and looked out.
> As I had hoped, the day was cloudless, a glorious
> morning. My first thought was *"Christ is risen!"*
> . . . There was a heavy white dew with a touch of
> hoar frost on the meadows, and as I leaned over the
> wicket gate by the millpond looking to see if there
> were any primroses in the banks but not liking to
> venture into the dripping grass, suddenly I heard
> the cuckoo for the first time this year . . . It is
> very well to hear the cuckoo for the first time on
> Easter Sunday morning.

That, like the appearance of banks of primroses,
and green swards covered with crocus flowers, is a
sign that we never know on this side of the world
as part of our Easter Celebration. But this token of
Life from seeming Death is the more telling, just for
that – when it is such a surprise on a visit to England!
Then, every country chapel and church offers this
unmistakable sign of New Life!

My Favourite Easter Affirmation Lives On!

> Look, Father, look on His anointed face
>   And only look on us as found in Him;
> Look not on our mis-usings of Thy grace,
>   Our prayer so languid, and our faith so dim.
> *For lo! between our sins and their reward*
>   *We set the passion of Thy Son, our Lord!*
>
> William Bright

* * * *

The world's first Easter Day brought to us what Dr Will Sangster rejoiced to call "the most glorious dawn in human history"! And no one ever queried his right to call it that, either in his great English congregations, Sunday by Sunday, Easter by Easter, or in my own little land, on the earth's far side, which he visited, on the strength of an eager invitation to preach. Since then a visit to London for a conference allowed him to call me to the platform; and for an exchange of books. His own book *Westminster Sermons*, Volume 2, lies open before me at this moment, and uses the very Easter-dawn phrase I have quoted. It speaks about the stone, set at the door of the Tomb, to which the sorrowing women came so early, bearing their spices. Mark and Luke tell us it was *"very early in the morning"*; Matthew says it was *"as it began to dawn"*; and John, *"when it was yet dark"*. All saying the same thing, really – and all concerned for their dilemma – *Who would roll away the stone?* For, as Will Sangster wrote, "there was no man in the party – and the stone was very great". But when they arrived, *"the stone was rolled away"*.

My preacher friend adds something that I have never heard anyone say before: "I think I know why. It was not rolled away that He might come out, but that they might go in . . . That they might steal into the empty tomb, and see *only 'the place where they laid Him'*." God was still in charge of the whole spiritual, physical issue!

Reading

For it was not very long – as we moderns count Earth years – before Christians of the Early Church had Paul writing to them in Corinth:

> *Now is Christ risen from the dead,*
>   and become the firstfruits of them that slept.
> For since by man came death,
>   by man came also the resurrection of the dead,
> For this corruptible must put on incorruption,
>   and this mortal must put on immortality.
>   O death, where is thy sting?
>   O grave, where is thy victory?
>   1 Corinthians 15:20, 21, 53, 55; A.V.

* * * *

Morning Prayer

O Lord of Life, it seems no time since I put out my light;
And now give Thee thanks for a new day.
   I would not be unmindful of the aged, and the sick,

who have no eager plans to bring to this day's
beginning;

I pray this morning for any newly come to retirement,

who have not as yet any new purpose for the day's
hours;

Give them a lively concern for others near at hand,
and eyes to see where they might offer a little help,
and kindness.

And let those of us still possessed of strength
of body and mind, "pull our weight" in the
affairs of home.

And bring us without regrets, to this day's end.
for Christ's sake.   AMEN.

R.F.S.

* * * *

A Morning Prayer

Gracious Father, I rejoice in the light of this new day;

For grass, and gardens, and for trees reaching high
overhead.

Save me from carelessness where others about me
are concerned.

Give me a generous spirit, that I may share what I
enjoy — any good news that reaches me this day,
in any way; any laughter;

Give me good judgement today, where I am required
to make a choice.

Give me courage to enter into new ventures that
will help folk.

Let me not magnify the faults of others in conversation;

And bless me with essential patience. For Christ's sake. AMEN.

R.F.S.

* * * *

Gracious God, I confess to a measure of carelessness at times; forgive me all unreasonable haste in human relationships. Let me show love, and a gentle sense of responsibility. In Christ's service. AMEN.

R.F.S.

The Surprise of Spring

A CELEBRATION ON A DATE AGREED
Have you ever heard a small child ask her Mother,
"Mummie, now that Spring's here, does that little
tree, just as big as me, with new green leaves all
over, feel pretty as we walk by?"

Well, does it? All I can say is, "I've been about
now for lots of Springs – but there are still questions
for which I don't have answers. That's part of the
surprise of Spring."

★ ★ ★ ★

Morning Prayer is On My Lips Again
Great Creator, I praise Thee for the beauty I find
out of doors;
    for new life that rises from tiny seeds;
    and green trees towering high with strength and
        shade.
I praise Thee, too, for fragrances hidden in secret
    places;
    "It is good," as the Psalmist says, "to sing praises
        to Thy name, O Most High;
    to declare Thy steadfast love in the morning,
        and Thy faithfulness by night."
Let me go about my affairs this day, with my
    eyes wide open,
    and my heart continually responsive, I pray.
AMEN.

R.F.S.

* * * *

And Again!

From the beginning of Time, kindred spirits have gloried in the Spring. Away back, in the pages of our Old Testament, we have the beautiful little Spring-song of the lover in "The Song of Solomon". His dear love has been carried away, and is detained in the court of the king. Miles and miles of cruel distance stretch between them.

It is Springtime – and he cannot bear it – this lovely mating time in the wide world around him.

And he seeks out words for a little song: *"Arise, my love, my fair one, and come away!"*

* * * *

And Yet Again!

Ever since God set the Miracle of Spring in our midst, it has been so – and will continue, we trust, unalloyed!

Away back, before mankind counted Time, and filled it with a thousand "urgent hurries", as we do today, Bartholomanseus Anglicus wrote:

Spring is the time of gladness and of love;
for in Spring tyme all thynge seemeth gladde,
for the earth wexeth grene, trees burgynne and
spred, meddowes bring forth flowers, heven
shyneth.

* * * *

The coming and going of many Springs has changed

the spelling of many words, but nothing of the essential loveliness of the Season itself.

We have Eleanor Farjeon, of our day, coming to us with "A Morning Song":

Morning has broken
Like the first morning;
Blackbird has spoken
Like the first bird.
   Praise for the singing,
   Praise for the morning,
   Praise for them, springing
From the first word!

Sweet the rain's new fall
Sunlit from heaven,
Like the first dewfall
On the first grass.
   Praise for the sweetness
   Of the wet garden,
   Sprung from completeness
Where His feet pass.

Mine is the sunlight,
Mine is the morning
Born of the one light
Eden saw play.
   Praise with elation,
   Praise every morning,
   God's re-creation
Of the new day.
               Eleanor Farjeon (1881–1965)

The Surprise of Spring

Gerard Manley Hopkins (1844–89) was happily aware of a Spring joy!

Nothing is so beautiful as Spring—
When weeds in wheels, shoot long and lovely and
    lush,
Thrush's eggs look like little low heavens, and
    thrush
Through the echoing timber does so rinse and
    wring
The ear, it strikes like lightnings to hear him sing;
The glassy pear tree leaves and blooms, they brush
The descending blue; that blue is all in a rush
With richness; the racing lambs too have fair their
    fling!

* * * *

My good Canadian poet-friend has a like joy in new lambs, and kindly permits me to share with you, what she has shared with me, of that Spring-time experience. Her charming poem she has titled "Bottle-Fed Lamb".

Hunger is real, and this
Delicious flow
That soothes the ravening,
Real also.
Held in the careful arms
Of the farmer's child,
He and his strange new world
Are reconciled.

His bunting cousins nudge
The natural source,
Pressing against their dams,
Matter-of-course.
He greedily devours
Life's recompense
And does not know the taste
Of difference.

R. H. Grenville

* * * *

And the wonder of it all is that Spring, in our earth life, is more than larks and lambs! More even than bright skies and bursting buds! Eight hundred and more years ago, a man unknown by name rejoiced in this, and sang:

The Earth's aflame again
With flowers bright.
The fields are green again,
The shadows deep,
Woods are aleaf again,
There is no living thing
That is not gay again,
With face of light
Garbed with delight,
Love is re-born,
And beauty wakes from sleep!

* * * *

And today another "unknown" sings as joyously — if briefly:

The Surprise of Spring

Triumphant news – a miracle I sing —
The everlasting miracle of Spring!

* * * *

And we must not close this celebration of the
surprise of Spring without climaxing its JOY with
the greatest Miracle of all – *the Spiritual reality that
Easter brings to us* year by year, as St Clement put it
long ago: *"The Christian life is a perpetual Springtime!"*

In Britain, as in those parts of the world where
Easter-tide – with its glorious message of Christ's
Rising from the Dead, into *a New, and more wonderful Life* – comes in with Spring, in the earth, about
homes and churches, LIFE FROM DEATH can be
a more easily-grasped REALITY!

* * * *

The assurance of our LIVING LORD is ever with
us: *"Because I live, ye shall live also"* (John 14:19).
It seems, to some of us, perhaps not much to say;
but, coming from Him, IT IS ALL WE NEED TO
KNOW!

"There is nothing in the world," said the beloved,
level-headed, trusted William Temple, a former
Archbishop of Canterbury, "of which I feel so
certain.

"I have no idea what it will be like, and I
am glad that I have not. I do not want it as a
mere continuance . . . 'God is love' appears to me
nonsense, in view of the world He has made, *if there
is no other!"*

* * * *

135

And there was nothing unexpected about that –
countless other great spirits have said the same,
up through the long centuries, including St John
of Damascus, whose words speak to us Easter by
Easter:

> *'Tis the Spring of souls today;*
>   Christ hath burst His prison,
> And from three days' sleep in death,
>   As the sun hath risen;
> All the winter of my sins,
>   Long and dark, is flying
> From His light, to Whom we give
>   Laud and praise undying!

> St John of Damascus,
> translated by J. M. Neale

★ ★ ★ ★

To Read, and Maybe Memorize, as Thanksgiving
  God of our life, through all the circling years,
    We trust in Thee;
  In all the past, through all our hopes and fears,
    Thy hand we see.
  With each new day when morning lifts the veil,
  We own Thy mercies, Lord, which never fail.

> Hugh Thomson Kerr

Once, and Now Forever

ASCENSION DAY

The largest gift parcel ever lodged in my sizeable letterbox came to me from London, and very supportive it has proved, from the moment of its arrival. *Collins English Dictionary* has sixteen-hundred-and-ninety two-columned pages! My only hope is that I'll still be able to lift the monster volume in old age! It's a joy! Scarcely a day goes by when we don't have happy dealings with each other!

I've just turned to "my good friend", to see what it has to say about ASCENSION DAY – and was happily surprised to find it starting off, like a good Christian, with a text (Acts 1:9), the like of which is not present in any of my several other smaller dictionaries, now "dog-eared". But that unexpected text is somehow reassuring, when it tells me that the Day is celebrated for a Christian reason – *to mark the passing of Jesus Christ from earth into heaven*. And the day allotted is the fortieth day after Easter. That, of course, was not news to me; but when I am dealing with a date, I do like "some learned volume" kindly to confirm it! My kind of books, it's now plain to me, have an eager way of finding readers both "handy-by" and "at the ends of the earth"! Countless letters arrive, commenting on the fact.

We men and women of this day and age ought to be able to take in any surprising, though sensible concept of earth, and heaven – essential to this long-established celebration.

In our present lifetime, we have certainly seen some remarkable sights ourselves – planes flying overhead any ordinary day; and with more preparation and fuss, men setting off for the Moon and, what must be counted even more amazing – returning unharmed, with photographs of the terrain, and rock-pieces in their bags, to prove it all true!

* * * *

But earlier – long before any of our clever air experts were even born, ordinary men and women in a little country of this earth, Palestine, witnessed an even more wonderful happening! That gives us, at this time of Ascension, *a remarkable reason* for celebration: the ascension – for the first time ever – of a young man from this earth to heaven – *our Lord and Master*! He went without "count-down" and "blast off", as the Moon-men were to know in our day, and His friends saw "a cloud receive Him out of their sight". That is how they spoke of it afterward, as it is recorded in the New Testament, to this day. In the familiar act of blessing them, He whom they knew, and loved, rose into heaven, and His followers – as Dr Luke recorded the experience told to him – "returned to Jerusalem *with great joy*". Not great fear, or great disappointment – but joy! (Luke 24:40–52; A.V.).

* * * *

In some ways, I think that the young man Jesus

must have been relieved from "comings and goings" on Earth! I've held that conviction a long time – ever since I was still a small schoolgirl, and shy. One day, a new teacher turned up, to take the place of our "real teacher", away with the 'flu. From the little semicircle standing before her, for some reason she put her first question of the first day, to me: "What is Geography?" For a moment, there was silence – then I put my answer into words that I've remembered ever since: "Please Miss, Geography is a very great bother!" Some of the girls giggled. She turned quickly to them – and somehow, I knew she was "on my side". "Would it be too hard to explain?" were her next words, and her voice softened.

"Geography is so big – all pieces of land – and so far!" I answered. At Sunday school we'd heard the story of Jairus, the ruler of the synagogue, with his little daughter, and his message to Jesus, saying how very sick she was, asking *Him to come quickly, and heal her!* (But you know the story – it was a long way; and Jesus was hindered by an old, very sick lady. As Jesus and His friends were walking to Jairus's house, they met her, and at once she told Him of her long-time troubles. She had been to lots of doctors – none of whom could heal her – and she'd been dreadfully sick for years. It took a long time to tell of it. But as soon as Jesus drew near, she pushed her way to Him, through the crowd.) Before Jesus and His friends could go on, a messenger came hurrying from the home of Jairus to say that the little girl had died. Yet Jesus decided to go on, and to lay His hand on her. There was a great crowd by the time they arrived, and many were crying loudly. It was a very sad scene.

But Jesus, led by the worried parents, went in to her – and presently, He reached out His hand and, after all this delay – *He raised her!* (Mark 5:22: A.V. Read on).

And there were so many other places too – for instance, blind people like Bartimaeus sat, each with a begging bowl held out, helpless – begging to be healed. How could Jesus, at the time – wearing an earthly human body – get to them all? He was a man of Earth, like all the rest of us?

And then there came that wonderful Day, that we celebrate today: ASCENSION DAY! It's celebrated by many thankful hearts in the Church the world round, with Joy – that Jesus was delivered from the limiting "bother" of Geography!

★　★　★　★

Said Jesus, in words that find a cherished and glorious place in our New Testament (Matthew 28:19–20; A.V.): "Go ye therefore, and teach all nations . . . teaching them to observe all things whatsoever I have commanded you: and, lo, *I am with you alway*, even unto the end of the world."

Dr William Barclay went on to enlarge on this in his book: *The Acts of the Apostles* (The Saint Andrew Press, Edinburgh).

The Ascension is not a conception of which we have any cause to be hesitant or doubtful. For two reasons the Ascension was *an absolute neces-*

sity. First, it was necessary that there be one final moment when Jesus did go back to the glory which was His. The forty days of the resurrection appearances had passed. Clearly, that was a time which was unique, and could not go on forever. Now equally clearly, the end to that period had to be definite.

Words spoken by "two men in white apparel . . ." (Acts 1:10–11; A.V.) were:

"Ye men of Galilee, why stand ye gazing up into heaven? This same Jesus, which is taken up from you into heaven, shall so come in like manner as ye have seen Him go into heaven." From these few words of Scripture, some men and women have been led, it seems, to enlarge to fantastic lengths their understanding of those two heavenly messengers.

★ ★ ★ ★

Dr Luke finishes his Gospel with a reminder of the joy that Jesus's parting words on that occasion of Ascension brought to those gathered about Him.

"I send the promise of My Father upon you," are His words; "but tarry ye in the city of Jerusalem, until ye be endued with power from on high." And He led them out as far as to Bethany, and He lifted up His hands, and blessed them. And it came to pass, while He blessed them, He was parted from them, and carried up into heaven. And they worshipped Him, and returned to Jerusalem with *great Joy.*

And were continually in the Temple, praising and blessing God. AMEN.

Luke 24:40–53; A.V.

There was no loneliness there – and no fear – only Joy and Blessing!

One Christian, of an unknown time, says with sweet certainty:

> I am not alone
> By night,
> Or by day,
> Or by circumstances;
> Neither in the silence,
> Nor in the city's roar!

Don't you think this is a supportive thing to be able to say? Really, a wonderful thing? I do.

And this unknown Christian as joyfully adds:

> Nor as I lie
> At the door of Death,
> Or stand on the
> threshold
> Of a new life;
> For Thou art with me.

"The Gospel *without the Resurrection*" – that we shared so joyously at Easter-tide, says Dr A. M. Ramsay, for Christians of our day – "*is not a gospel* at all – not merely a gospel without its final chapter."

And of the Ascension, every one of us must say the same!

142

Reading For Any Day

Who shall separate us from the love of Christ? shall tribulation, or distress, or persecution, or famine, or nakedness, or peril, or sword? As it is written, For thy sake we are killed all the day long: we are accounted as sheep for the slaughter.

Nay, in all these things, we are more than conquerors through Him that loved us.

For I am persuaded, that neither death, nor life, nor angels, nor principalities, nor powers, nor things present, nor things to come, nor height, nor depth, nor any other creature, shall be able to separate us from the love of God, which is in Christ Jesus our Lord.

Romans 8:35–39; A.V.

★ ★ ★ ★

A Modern Cause of Gratitude

To be glad of life, because it gives you the chance to love and to work and to play and to look up at the stars, to be satisfied with your possessions, but not contented with yourself until you have made the best of them, to despise nothing in the world except falsehood and meanness, and to fear nothing except cowardice, to be governed by your admirations rather than my your disgusts, to covet nothing that is your neighbour's except his kindness of heart and gentleness of manners, to think seldom of your enemies, often of your friends, and *every day of Christ*, and to spend as much time as you can, with body and with spirit, in God's out-of-doors, these are little guideposts on the footpath to peace.

Henry van Dyke

Celebrating a Big Birthday

THE FEAST OF PENTECOST

This, you must know, is not just a well organized occasion in your home or mine – for all that it is a joy when somebody there adds another year to life! *This*, is worldwide – once every year – *and there's no other like it!*

It's the birthday of the World Church! Those who don't join in have missed something unmatched!

It was first given with *the Gift of the Holy Spirit*! And that's not something you can secretly wrap up in pretty paper, and slip in by the back door! Not at all, not at all!

It came first, when a little company of Christians of the first century gathered in Jerusalem, by instruction of their Master *"to wait"* – they hardly knew for what.

Pick up your New Testament – the account is fascinatingly written of there by Dr Luke, after he had finished his lovely Gospel, that's been so long a favourite. In Acts, chapter 2, it begins with as much expectation, and as little certain knowledge, as any birthday ever began on this earth. (Read about it.) "And when the day of Pentecost was fully come, they were all with one accord in one place . . ." It sounds like a birthday celebration, doesn't it? And of course it was! Now read on!

"We may never know precisely what happened on the day of Pentecost," says Dr William Barclay, "but we do know that it was one of the supremely great days of the Christian Church, for on that day the Holy Spirit came to the Christian Church in a very special way.

"It is perhaps unfortunate that we so often speak of the events of Pentecost as *the coming of the Holy Spirit.* The danger is that we think that the Holy Spirit came into existence at that time. Now that is not so; God is *eternally* Father, Son and Holy Spirit. In point of fact, Acts makes that quite clear. The Holy Spirit was speaking in David (Acts 1:16). The Spirit spoke through Isaiah (Acts 28:25); Stephen in his speech accuses the Jews of having, all through their history, opposed the Spirit (Acts 7:51). In that sense the Spirit is God *in every age*, and in every generation revealing His truth, and His will to men. Yet at the same time, *something special* happened at Pentecost.

"*From that moment, the Holy Spirit became the dominant reality in the life of the early Church.* For one thing, the Holy Spirit was *the source of all guidance* . . . [of meetings with fellow missionary workers, for instance (R.F.S.)]] And opening up of new work: and very importantly, the men of the Church were all *'men of the Spirit'.*"

Dr Barclay finishes with a wonderful general summary, when he says, "All the members of the Early Church lived in the Spirit, as they lived in the very air which they breathed." In Dr Barclay's memory, at that moment of writing, was an important passage in Acts, which he had been studying, with its threefold reference to *God* the Father; *Jesus* the Son; and (as set out in Acts, 5:30–32) "*the Holy Spirit*, whom God hath *given to them that obey Him*". (*A very striking condition*, isn't it?)

★　★　★　★

In many of our church hymnbooks is a hymn which says:

> So when the Spirit of our God
>   Came down His flock to find,
> A voice from Heaven was heard abroad,
>   A rushing mighty Wind.
>
> It fills the Church of God; it fills
>   The sinful world around;
> Only in stubborn hearts and wills
>   No place for it is found.

John Keble

Yes, obedience counts for much!

Edwin Hatch shared his deeply desired prayer-hymn:

> Breathe on me, breath of God,
>   Fill me with Life anew,
> That I may love what Thou dost love,
>   And do what Thou wouldst do.
>
> Breathe on me, Breath of God,
>   Until my heart is pure,

Until with Thee I will one will,
   To do and to endure.

Yes . . . God is lovingly hopeful of my obedience!

"Brother Anonymous" and his kin are undoubtedly the busiest verse-lovers in our world. We are never able to thank any one of them, though occasionally we would like to. (Whilst pondering on this page, I came across a verse headed "Upon the Day of Pentecost", and felt it ought to go in here, as a summary.)

Upon the day of Pentecost
The Holy Spirit came —
Like powerful, rushing, mighty wind
And leaping, living flame.

The friends of Jesus till that hour
Were fearful folk and weak;
But now the *Holy Spirit* made
Them bold and wise to speak.

With joy and confidence they went
To all whom they could reach,
In God the Holy Spirit's power
To praise and heal and teach.

God's Holy Spirit still is here
To guide our world today,
*And helps the friends of Jesus Christ
In what they do and say.*

* * * *

The glorious key-verse that comes to my heart and mind constantly as a Christian, is the eighth verse of the first chapter of the New Testament book of Acts, spoken both to humble people and to great, transformed on the first birthday celebration of the World Church:

> You shall receive power when the Holy Spirit has come upon you; and you shall be *my witnesses* in *Jesuralem* and in all *Judea* and *Samaria*, and *to the end of the Earth* (Revised Standard Version).

This started exactly *where they were*, in Jerusalem; then went out *to the next place*; then *to the next*, still further out; *then further still* – to the end of the Earth! And that's where we come in today! What that eighth verse is saying – in whatever version you read it, is – "this Christian witness, in actuality – whoever you are or where – is *"the biggest thing on earth!"*

★ ★ ★ ★

A Prayer to Add to My Own
Gracious, Eternal Father, we bless Thee! You gladden our hearts, and set us to witness to Christ Jesus, our Lord, wherever we are – wherever we go – as long as life lasts!
We cannot think of anything worse than to fail in this; anything better than to *do* Your will in Your world!   Amen.

R.F.S.

★ ★ ★ ★

Speaking with tongues is, as I see it, not on its own

proof of the presence of the Spirit; but witness of a Christ-like love in one's day-to-day life is. The place where this begins first of all is in one's surrendered personality – which wakens lovelier, more loyal!

My Scottish preacher-author friend, Dr J. S. Stewart – from whom rich years have brought me many letters, and with whom, a little while ago, I was guest at a shared meal, and a long talk before a mutual friend's fire – says in a book:

Always there are unmistakable signs when the power of the Spirit goes to work . . . when a man, ["or a woman" I add] once weak and shifty and unreliable, becomes strong and clean and victorious; when a church once stagnant and conventional and introverted, throws off its dull tedium, and catches fire, and becomes alert and missionary-minded; when Christians of different denominations begin to realize there is far more in the Risen Christ to unite them than there can be anywhere else in the world, or in their tradition, to divide them; when religion, too long taboo in polite conversation, becomes a talking point again; when decisions for Christ are seen worked out in family and business relationships; when mystic vision bears fruit in social passion – then indeed, the world is made to know that something is happening.

★ ★ ★ ★

Today, I would celebrate God's kindled Flame —

with colours blended;

His Wind – with feelings given power;
I would adventure forth
  into Earth's ways,
with valiant courage, and gentleness,
supporting every living soul with respect,
sending no child loveless to bed.

R.F.S.

God will, in these modern days, do – as He can, through my *witness* to the Faith. *"What is a witness?"* asks William Barclay, rejoicing in the New Testament men and women involved in the birthday of the Church. And then he answers it, joyously: "A witness is a person who says, *"This is true and I know it!"*

  From *God's Young Church*, by William Barclay
(The Saint Andrew Press)

Not So Simple, Perhaps?

TRINITY SUNDAY

The day comes round, and preachers preach, but
not all the pew-holders, I fear, have a clear idea of
what Trinity Sunday is all about. As far as preachers
go, I can only give them the benefit of the doubt,
though the only one I actually know of who spoke
"plainly of this part of his position" – if you can call
it "plain" – was an old, black preacher, who began his
sermon: "Brothers and sisters, this morning I intend
to ponder the imponderable, define the indefinable,
and unscrew the inscrutable."

In one of his Trinity Sunday sermons, my London
friend, Dr W. E. Sangster, during his distinguished
ministry in Westminster said:

> I remember, many years ago, following three
> children out of morning worship from a Sussex
> village chapel. It was Trinity Sunday. The girl was
> aged about fourteen, and the boys about twelve
> and ten.
>
> The elder boy said to his sister: "I can't under-
> stand all this 'three in one and one in three'
> business."
>
> "I can't understand it either," she said, "but I
> think of it this way. Mother is 'Mumma' to me;
> she is 'Mabel' to Daddy; and she is 'Mrs Douglas'
> to lots of other people . . ."

"Is that the answer then?" asked my friend. "Is it just a question of names?" And as quickly, and assuredly, he answered, "*No!* It is deeper than that – adroit as the little girl was in finding an analogy which could help her through childhood.

"The doctrine of the Holy Trinity is nowhere mentioned under that name in Scripture – though the doctrine is clearly there by implication. We have come to the central mystery of the Christian faith, and we may as well settle with ourselves as we begin this sermon," he went on to his listeners, "that we shall not *fully* understand the mystery, at the end.

"Not," went on my friend, "that that need depress us unduly! It is commonly agreed among all who believe in God, that 'a God comprehended, is no God'. Could a Being fully understood by mortals *be* God? We should expect – not the irrational, certainly – but just as certainly, the unfathomable; a deep where all our thoughts are drowned.

"But let us venture forward! It is Trinity Sunday again, the only great day in the Christian year not associated with an event, *but purely with doctrine.*

"So when the record was set down man already had clear concepts. He could say, 'God'." The Bible opens with "In the beginning, God . . ."

★   ★   ★   ★

Talking it over with an honoured theologian, a neighbour and friend of mine, Dr J. J. Lewis, now retired Principal of Trinity College, New Zealand, he turned my attention to a passage in a little theological book he took pleasure in giving me, *Between The Vision and The Word* (College Communications, St John's Road, Auckland. N.Z.).

For Trinity Sunday I take pleasure in sharing a brief quotation:

> Here all Christian insights flow together. Across the centuries there have been so many fluctuating emphases. The Church did not want to leave anything out of its response to *God, as Source of all life.* [From the beginning, as I set it down humbly for myself – *God the Creator,* and Father of our human spirits.] This is a big thing to say – but our life here on Earth, and at any time, anywhere – would be impossible, without this reality.
>
> *And the Second Person of the Trinity* is God in history – that is, set among us in Earth time – *Jesus,* of Whom we read much in the New Testament – and Whose footprints we cross the world to trace, as we believe is possible, in Palestine. The Holy Land is much changed through the centuries, but still offering us Bethlehem, where He was born – within sight of The Shepherds' Fields; Nazareth – with its well, and the setting for His early life, and manhood toil as a carpenter. A town whose streets men and women, including ourselves, have walked ever since, and to which, with a sound village craftsman's record in business, He feared not to return, at the very start of His Ministry, as God Incarnate: *to be Healer, Master, Saviour.*
>
> *And the Third Person of the Trinity* – in the words

of Dr J. J. Lewis, reverently repeated in conversation, and in his little book, is experienced as God the Holy Spirit – *"God in you and me"*.

* * * *

So the early Church came to say: *"God the Father; God the Son; God the Holy Ghost*. Three Persons, but One God."

Three in One. God above us; God among us; God within us. God in origins; God in history; God in experience.

* * * *

"It is Trinity Sunday," said Dr Sangster one memorable Sunday at Westminster Central Hall, when I worshipped there. *"We are at the central mystery of our most holy Faith. Let us adore the Great Triune God!"*

* * * *

For Trinity Sunday, a Prayer
Almighty and Eternal God, Holy Father, we bless Thee that Thou hast shined in our hearts to give the light of the knowledge of Thy glory in the face of Jesus Christ, and hast bestowed upon us through Him the gift of Thy Holy Spirit, that He should dwell with us and be in us. Grant that we, receiving this revelation of Thyself, may know and worship Thee aright, the one triune God and Lord, to Whom be glory for ever and ever.   Amen.

Divine Worship

* * * *

Not So Simple, Perhaps?

The Collect for the First Sunday after Trinity
O God, the strength of all them that put their trust in Thee, mercifully accept our prayers; and because through the weakness of our mortal nature we can do no good thing without Thee, grant us the help of Thy grace, that in the keeping of Thy commandments we may please Thee, both in will and deed; through Jesus Christ our Lord.   Amen.

The Book of Common Prayer

The words of George Wallace Briggs' hymn are with me at this moment:

> God has spoken by Christ Jesus,
> Christ, the everlasting Son,
> brightness of the Father's glory,
> with the Father ever one;
> spoken by the Word incarnate,
> God from God, ere time began,
> Light from Light, to earth descending,
> Man, revealing God to man.
>
> God is speaking by His Spirit,
> speaking to the hearts of men,
> in the age-long word expounding
> God's own message, now as then,
> through the rise and fall of nations
> one sure faith yet standing fast;
> God still speaks, His word unchanging,
> God the first, and God the last.

George Wallace Briggs (1875–1958)

155

Intercession This Day

> Dear Lord, for all in pain
>   We pray to Thee;
> O come and smite again
>   Thine enemy.
> Give to Thy servants skill
>   To soothe and bless,
> And to the tired and ill
>   Give quietness.
> And, Lord, to those who know
>   Pain may not cease,
> Come near, that even so
>   They may have peace.   AMEN.
>   Amy Wilson Carmichael

Let Me Share Yet Another's Assurance

> And I smiled to think God's greatness
> Flowed around our incompleteness —
> Round our restlessness, His rest.
>   Elizabeth Barrett Browning

* * * *

"Even if a cloud hides the sun, I know the sun is still there and shining," says a Scottish writer of our day, Alistair Maclean. "If I cannot hear the music of the river among the high hills, I know that the river is still running blithely in the valley below me. And if mystery and sorrow and doubt and pain curtain the face of my Father's love and care, yet all my knowledge and experience tell me that *He still lives, and still loves me.*"

Psalm Ninety-five, to Memorize

O come, let us sing unto the Lord;
Let us make a joyful noise to the rock of our
    salvation.
Let us come before His presence with thanks-
    giving,
And make a joyful noise unto Him with psalms.
For the Lord is a great God,
And a great King above all gods.
In His hands are the deep places of the earth:
The strength of the hills is His also.
The sea is His, and He made it:
And His hands formed the dry land.
O come, let us worship and bow down:
Let us kneel before the Lord our Maker.
For He is our God:
And we are the people of His pasture, and the
    sheep of His hand.
Today if ye will hear His voice,
Harden not your hearts.

                                        Psalm 95: 1–8; A.V.

Two in Harmony

COVENANT SUNDAY

Some while ago, when travelling by myself, I was in a strange city, where I knew no one save a kindly couple I'd met at a Conference. They had invited me to stay at any time I found myself passing through – and this was the moment.

It so chanced that they were Methodist folk, and this was Covenant Sunday. I was sorry to be away from my own pew and congregation, but there was nothing I could do about it.

And, of course, it didn't matter really. They invited me to accompany them to Service in their own church, which I was happy to do. I was also happy that it *was* Covenant Sunday.

Long, long before, a little company of Christians had met John Wesley at the old gun foundry in Moorfields, which he had converted into the first Methodist Chapel. Later, that very day, Wesley took time to write in his *Journal*: "I strongly urged the wholly giving up ourselves to God, and renewing in every point *our covenant* that the Lord should be our God."

It was a historic moment, now remembered the world round in the Covenant Service we celebrate once a year. It is a very individual, and yet corporate experience, where – as part of the set Service – we are each encouraged to repeat sincerely:

I am no longer my own, but Thine. Put me to what Thou wilt: rank me with whom Thou wilt; put me to doing, put me to suffering; let me be employed for Thee or laid aside for Thee; let me be full, let me be empty; I freely and heartily yield all things to Thy pleasure and disposal. And now, O glorious and blessed God, Father, Son and Holy Spirit, Thou art mine and I am Thine. So be it. *And the Covenant which I have made on earth, let it be ratified in heaven.* Amen.

It is never an easy thing to repeat those solemn words either alone or in company with other believers, in this shared World, as we have it.

★ ★ ★ ★

But then, covenant-making can never have been an easy thing, right from the beginning – and its beginning, was, of course, very long ago. My dictionary has only one definition of a Covenant, religious, or otherwise, and it is: *"a binding agreement, a contract"*. My *Everyman's Encyclopaedia* – and this implies, of course, "*Everywoman's* Encyclopaedia", gives it as "mutual agreement made by two persons or groups of persons, or by a person or persons with their god or gods. The term (Hebrew *bérith*) is much used in the Old Testament for various kinds of agreements. They were looked upon as sacred and binding, the children of Israel being particularly forbidden to make any covenants with the Canaanites." (If you care to take the time, to turn up any average sized Concordance of The Bible, covering both Old and New Testaments, as these established works of reference do (and always, alas, in small type), you'll find hundreds of references in careful order. All were honoured in their day and setting, no doubt, and meaningful in the taxing moments of life.

But let me move on from what I have just written of the annual Covenant Service in the Methodist Church, to which I belong. Because I know sincerely – and to my enrichment – that the constant readers of my books are not, by any means, all Methodists. I get so many letters from readers all over the world. (I do my best to answer each one – and smartly – but it's not simple, though I love to hear of others' joy in reading. *And a writer is kept close to life that way*, by human people, practical people, generous people – gladsome in their judgements, some, unconsciously witty.

The first letter to reach me, was away back, when I was still doing story books for child readers, of whom a good number wrote to me. The very first was a little fellow of about nine, I would think. His teacher chanced to be a friend of mine, who sometimes came to stay with us in the holidays. One year, she passed on news that I'd had a misadventure on a dangerous set of steps, and was in hospital, with a damaged foot and ankle. The lad had the sense to ask her how to spell the name of my hospital. And that night, after tea, he wrote me a letter, which reached me next day in an envelope addressed in bold, block letters. His first words were: "I AM SORRY TO HEAR OF YOUR FATAL ACCIDENT." A day or so on, I got permission from my Ward Sister, to read it out to the five others with me there. And the chuckles that followed, did us all good!

Some months later, a letter from my Editor in London asked me to prepare a slender book on the beloved, beautiful, and gifted Susannah Wesley – Mother of the brothers John and Charles and the rest, not forgetting the sisters. And I went to Epworth, to stay a few nights in the old home of them all, which was being refurbished as a "Retreat House". And a great privilege it was to be there – even, on one special occasion, to be served a sit-down meal in Susannah's kitchen – and later, to handle her little prayerbook, similar to the copy I had at home in my study, on the far side of the world, of which she knew nothing. But I have – with others – all my life been blessed by what she did know. "Help me, Lord, to remember," she wrote in her little prayerbook, to which I often turn on Covenant Sunday, *"that religion is not confined to the Church or closet, nor exercised only in prayer and meditation*, but that everywhere I am in Thy presence."

MY OWN COVENANT PRAYER – SHARED FOR THE FIRST TIME – IS:

Gracious Lord and Father of my lasting spirit, nothing is so meaningful within this Earthlife, as to live assured of Thy Love and Mercy: nothing so poor and worthless, as to fail my side of this gracious Covenant. Help me! Hold me!   AMEN.

In the Methodist Hymn Book – the hymn book

that I handle most often throughout the world, is the section specially set for Covenant Services, with an early contribution by Charles Wesley, the hymn-loving son of Susannah. It begins:

> All praise to our redeeming Lord,
> Who joins us by His grace,
> And bids us each to each restored,
> *Together* to seek His face.
>
> He bids us build each other up;
> And gathered into one,
> To our high calling's hope
> We hand in hand go on.
>
> Charles Wesley

And next to it is another just as well-known, and *as personal*:

> I am Thine, O Lord; I have heard Thy voice,
> And it told Thy love to me;
> But I long to rise in the arms of faith,
> And be closer drawn to Thee.
>
> Consecrate me now to Thy service, Lord,
> By the power of Grace divine;
> Let my soul look up with a steadfast look,
> And my will be lost in Thine.
>
> Frances Jane van Alstune,
> a more recent hymnwriter

Though Covenant Services had long been a custom for Methodists on the first Sunday of the Year, it is still counted a precious experience.

"A Covenant," we say, "is a Covenant!" And sometimes raise our voices to add meaningfully:

> *We'll praise Him for all that is past*
> *And trust Him for all that's to come!*

*   *   *   *

A Reading at Day's End

He made the disciples get into the boat and go before Him to the other side. And after He had dismissed the crowds, He went up on the mountain by Himself, to pray. When evening came, He was there alone, but the boat by this time was many furlongs distant from the land, beaten by the waves, for the wind was against them.

And in the fourth watch of the night He came to them, walking on the sea . . . And they cried out for fear. But immediately, He spoke to them, saying: *"Take heart, it is I, have no fear."*

Matthew 14:22–27; R.S.V.

In correspondence with Percy Dearmer, he sent me, with permission to share it, his following lovely poem on hands:

> Now rest in abeyance
>   From market and mill
> Millions of hands
>   Unaware of their skill;
> Hands pale as faience,
>   Hands brown as hazel,
> How can I praise all

Those that are gifted?
Hands like the rose
  To the wild rose grafted,
How from such good
  Can I choose?
Some lovely food
  Have spicily garnished
(Sauces and stews);
  Others, nail varnished
Have tapped like the yaffle
  A texture of news.

Now sleep-arrested
  They lie on the pillow
Or clasped in a fellow,
  Or open, uncurled;
And some are as shell-pink
  As the silk petals
Of roses unfurled —
  The soft hands of children,
  The hope of the world.

Our Countless Saints

ALL SAINTS' DAY

As I leaf through my little red pocket diary, All Saints' Day greets me year by year, on 1st November, and I am strengthened and cheered, in that remembrance, no matter how busy I am – or how far from home, perhaps tired, on my travels. For I have learned to count on the company of the Saints.

"Saints?" do you say – "I'm not sure that I wouldn't sooner enjoy the company of sinners." And your derogatory reaction leaves me wondering where you've fashioned that unfortunate judgement. Can it be that the very word "saint" has come to belong to a drawn figure in a stained-glass window, with a useless halo of light bestowed by the Church? If so, what a pity!

Sir Hugh Walpole was more fortunate. "The only happy people I have ever known in my life," said he, "have been *saints* – my mother, a doctor, a clergyman, human beings who *lost themselves entirely in something larger than themselves.*"

★　★　★　★

It may be that you have been unfortunate in the people you've met. But it's more likely that no one until now has explained that the name "saint", as used in New Testament times, stood not for a perfect being – but for a forgiven sinner.

In the New Testament, the word for a thing spotless, was *hieros*; but *hagios* was the word for "saint", meaning *not* one with a perfect personality and record, but rather one — whatever his or her past record — who has *now* become wholly dedicated to God!

So there were "saints" in all sorts of likely, and unlikely, places, as will be plain to you, if you read through the headings, or the post-scripts, of Paul's many letters, as they have come down to us in the New Testament. For instance, "To all that be in Rome, beloved of God, *called to be saints*" ("The Epistle of Paul the Apostle to the Romans", chapter 1, verse 7). There were, surprisingly, "Saints in Caesar's *household*", to whom Paul sent greetings, in one of his letters written from Rome, and now in our New Testament in "The Epistle of Paul the Apostle to the Philippians" (Philippians 4:21–22; A.V.). "Salute every saint. The brethren which are with me greet you. *All the saints* salute you, chiefly they that are of Caesar's *household*." Not necessarily, modern scholars now assure us, actual blood relations or family folk, but former soldiers and government servants, slaves many of them, all with a background of hideous cruelty. (The very last setting in which to look for saints!)

★ ★ ★ ★

If you are fortunate enough to have a private copy of Professor Herbert Butterfield's fine *Christianity and Ministry*, as I am, or can get to the public library, you will never think ill of the word "saint" again.

But I am not forgetting the earnest, widely known petition of one who was herself a saint – the bright, cheerful Spanish nun, Saint Theresa. She felt she had to pray, from time to time, *"From silly devotions, and from sour-faced saints*, good Lord deliver us!"* – a prayer that must not be allowed to go out of circulation. You and I must see to that.

Someone spoke of the beloved Dr Bell, Bishop of Chichester, earlier in this century, as *"seeming a modern saint* par excellence – not retreating from the world", as it came to him in his lovely city setting, that I visited and enjoyed for a few days, before the War engulfed it. "And he went on accepting the world, with all its twentieth-century tensions." A long, steady witness!

And I like to mention one woman, as seeming to balance the record, Alice Meynell, home-maker, essayist, and sensitive Christian poet, "accustomed to walk in holy places, and keep the eye of a fresh mind on our entangled world". It was never my privilege to meet her – but I think there is nothing she wrote, and published for the rest of us, that I have not read.

There are still, to this moment, countless saints about!

★ ★ ★ ★

One Long Living Prayer to memorize
Lord of Life, we offer Thee most hearty thanks for the grace and virtue made manifest *in all Thy saints*, who have been chosen vessels of Thy favour, and lights of the world, in their several generations.   AMEN.

Origin unknown

I am just back from a fascinating visit to my Public Library, a place to which I go often. It is no great distance on foot, and I am often enriched by that fact. I have made some great "finds" there, and today, came on one I haven't seen for just on twenty years – published, in fact, by my own London publishers, Collins, in hardback. It was called by a striking hyphenated one-word title that might have put off some likely readers. But not me – I was curious to see what the enchanting American writer of verse and prose had made of her subject: "SAINT-WATCHING". *Today, I know* – and remember, the rich gift to life made by the modern saints I have here mentioned, not to overlook countless others. I knew that "Saint-Watching" in the flesh remains *one of this Life's greatest adventures!*

✳ ✳ ✳ ✳

Well on in his heroic missionary life among the boats and people of Labrador's rugged coasts, Dr Grenfell paid a visit to London, to share the story of his adventures with an eager rally of five thousand boys waiting for him.

Before they parted, he raised a hand above his head to say to those who had sat fascinated, "I dare not close without saluting my Chief. I owe everything I am to my Lord Jesus Christ. Forty years ago, I gave Him my allegiance, and *He gave me Himself, and with Himself the gift of everlasting Life.* Every day since He has since lived in me, and He has made me the sharer of His Spirit, and His Peace."

Thus spake – even as he lived – a modern day saint!

Saints spend no time searching for excuses in this hungry world. The writer of the following petition has not left his name – perhaps he was ashamed to, on reflection.

Don't ask us to feed the multitudes;
Our hands might suddenly
Smell of fish.
And crumbs would catch
In our trouser-cuffs.

Anon

A Japanese saint, whom it was my joy to meet, and hear speak – Kagawa, has left us a far more memorable statement:

. . . Today
A wonderful thought
In the dawn was given,
And the thought
Was this:
That a secret plan
Is hid in my hand;
That my hand is big,
Big,
Because of this plan.
That God,
Who dwells in my hand,
Knows this secret plan
Of the things He will do for the world
Using my hand!

Christmas – and Always

My Master's Everlasting Words for Me Today
I am come that men may have life, and may have it
in all its fulness! (John 10:10; New English Bible).
(And here the word *men* means *humanity* – men,
women and children.)

★　★　★　★

Morning Prayer
O God, I am glad to be alive – and here – at
　　the dawn of this new day. I bless Thee for this
　　wonderful world, in which I may serve in the
　　establishment of Thine Everlasting Kingdom.
Deliver me from the tyranny of trifles; let the
　　values of my Master, Christ, be uppermost in all
　　my daily plans. I need constantly a true sense of
　　perspective, and honest, unvarying purpose.
Let me realize, in all my human relationships, how
　　much more people matter than things. Enable us
　　to hear Thy call to us, *to be Thy Saints!*
Let me make time, and place, in my day, for
　　outreaching love to the sick, the sad, and the
　　stumbling. I name some especially, in this moment
　　of intercession —— and ——
Let my love be truly supportive – and not give
　　way to fussing. In the Name of Christ, Who
　　never failed to understand. And to encourage,
　　and forgive. AMEN.

R.F.S.

★　★　★　★

Evening Prayer
Eternal Father, Giver of Life, and of saintly com-

panionship, this night, in celebration of All Saints'
Day we bless Thee. We marvel that in Thy service,
the world round, there is room for us all.

We bless Thee for new experiences this day – for
new companionships, and new and helpful ideas.

We praise Thee for the beauty of this Earth; and
the courage, and goodness, and the liveliness of
so many who share it with us.

And we give thanks for the constant care that
so many display.

Forgive us, where we are careless, and casual,
where others struggle, and scarcely succeed.

We rejoice in every experience of helpful hospitality;
for every token of concern.

Hold us all in Thy holy keeping. For Christ's
sake.   AMEN.

R.F.S.

* * * *

A Psalm to Share
*"Sing unto the Lord, O ye saints of His, and give
thanks at the remembrance of His holiness!"*

(Psalm 30:4; A.V.)

Harvest Is Here!

HARVEST THANKSGIVING

From early eager growing-up days on the farm right until now, I've never heard any doubt about the fittingness of "Harvest Festival" celebrations. Though it seems that some have: early on, certain playful young Anglican priests, I'm told, referred to the festival in private as "The Feast of *St Pumpkin, and All Marrows*".

Certainly with us, year by year, the celebration was one that we never missed. In a sense, it started for some of us on Saturday, when, young and old, we went round small gardens and farms collecting up waiting sheaves of golden corn, fruits and flowers of the best, to decorate the Chapel for the next day's Thanksgiving. We could be sure of one of the year's largest congregations on that day!

One of the earliest Bible verses we learned at home, and listened to annually from the pulpit, was Genesis 1, verse 11: "God said, 'Let the Earth bring forth grass and herb yielding seed, and the fruit tree yielding fruit after his kind . . .' " followed by verse 12: *"And the earth brought forth fruit . . . and God saw that it was good."*

It was "good" to us, too – and joyous! Especially so on one particular Sunday, with the Chapel just opened after the previous afternoon's decoration, its harvest scents confined sweetly in the closed building till opening time, when the eager congregation entered. And along with it, this time, our neighbour Geordie Millar's old wandering pig – attracted by the sweet scents, just liberated! When two stewards rose to pull it back down the aisle, we all learned that a pig with sharp hoofs wasn't built to reverse under pressure. It had to be led forward, into a space where it could turn, made by the removal of a few marrows, pumpkins, and bags of apples, so that "the creature" could turn and be brought back down the aisle, face-on!

Then we were soon restored to our serious Thanksgiving, with the hymn:

Come, ye thankful people, come,
Raise the song of Harvest Home;
All is safely gathered in,
Ere the Winter storms begin!

And we were thankful to God, by whose ancient powers it was so! We humble farm folk never forgot our human limitations. Our Service was, in very truth, *a Celebration of Thanksgiving*!

* * * *

Never a month of the year passes on this Earth, but somewhere Harvest is in full swing, gathered in by the sweat of the brow by thankful folk. My own little country, New Zealand, leads off with an in-gathering in sunny January. Chile joins us in this; parts of India and Upper Egypt follow in February and March. The remainder of India's harvest is gathered in April. Syria, Asia Minor, and Persia follow on, in May.

June brings in the harvest of Italy, Spain, Turkey, and Southern France. Harvest extends over three months in the wide-spread United States of America. South Russia gathers in her harvest in July, as do farmers in Bulgaria, Rumania, Hungary and Germany. Central Russia, Poland, Canada, and England gather in during August and September. The same months also see an in-gathering in Northern Russia. October shifts the scene to Sweden and Norway. November brings harvesters of South Africa into the fields, and the year is at last rounded out with the harvesting of Australia, Argentina and Abyssinia. So every month – somewhere in the great, round world – men and women are helping to answer the prayer for bread. This is God's good way – He does not easily put bread into our outreached hands without effort on our part.

Many of the sturdiest peoples eat only brown bread, or even black,. In the Middle Ages it was known as "maslin bread" – made of rye chiefly, along with some wheat. In other countries, it had an addition of barley and oats.

And bread of all shades has been continually toiled for, and prayed for, as well as individually and collectively rejoiced in together annually, at Harvest Thanksgiving Celebrations!

This cannot be bypassed, even in these days of modern tractors, fertilizers and new agricultural skills, for farmers – as they well know – are still dependent on God for sun, rain, and growth, wherever they find themselves with "an area of earth"!

It is essential that they keep this in mind, and

share the outcome with their fellows in the rest
of the world's country places, villages, towns, and
cities. Today many constantly go to bed hungry ,
and rise hungry to face each new day. These, sad
to say, add up to millions — whilst at the same time
there are countless others who overeat. *All in the same
world!*

Happily, there are others, not only at Harvest
time, but all the year round, who regularly fast one
day a week, in order to make gifts toward digging
wells in parched areas, and sharing food in places,
where today many continually hunger. It would be
wonderful if those church people, and all others in
work, who never miss a meal, and who think of
their fellows in need, could be vastly multiplied *in
God's name!*

> The first bread I tasted, came from my Mother's
>   oven,
> gold-crusted, sweetest of the gifts of Earth,
> made from the best flour, from the best grain
> grown in the sun-blessed countryside that gave
>   me birth.

R.F.S.

*Harvest Festival reminds me of my obligations. It cannot
be otherwise!*

★ ★ ★ ★

Another Harvest Prayer
Gracious Lord, and Father, I bring Thee thanks for
     my little bit of Earth, in which to grow things;
And for many meal-time needs, met by the unselfish

175

sharing of others – for Thy Namesake.
Grant me, till my life's end, I pray, a like spirit.   AMEN.

R.F.S.

★   ★   ★   ★

And Another – that Seed-time and Harvest Fail Not
Father of mercies, and Author of all good, Whose
providence for Thy children never faileth, and
Whose continual blessings are unnumbered, grant
that we may so live in the fellowship of Thy
family, that *we may together enjoy Thy bounty
with rejoicing hearts*: through Jesus Christ our
Lord.   AMEN.

R.F.S.

★   ★   ★   ★

A Prayer Out of Doors
For the simple things I often take for granted,
   O God —
I give you thanks now;
For the immensity of the sky,
For the fertility of the earth,
For water with reflections or dashing-smashing
beauty,
   and always life-giving powers;
For the song of birds,
For the natural movement of wild creatures,
For crickets and grasshoppers, and the gauzy wings
   of dragonflies;
For the graceful curves of grass stalks,
For the changing colours of leaves,

Harvest Is Here!

For the cleansing, refreshing might of winds;
For the purity and challenge of mountain peaks.
For the awesomeness of thunder,
For the unceasing power and pull of the tides.
Above all these, I give thanks that You have
   placed in my personality secrets whose issue is
   in Eternity, power to worship You, to love You,
   and to serve You, now and always.

A Woman's Book of Prayers

Whilst in Another's Company, I Was Permitted Lately to Share a Confession

   This is our poverty
   That we do not belong to each other,
   Nor serve one another.
   We go each his own way
   And do not care for our neighbour.
   We pray Thee, O Lord,
   Redeem us from this estrangement,
   Deliver us from the sin that divides us,
   Join us closely in true Love.

In another of his "opening sentences", my friend
Dr Sangster said in one of his Harvest Sermons:

   So far as Thanksgiving is concerned, the mass of
   people can be divided into two classes: those who
   take things *for granted*, and those who take things
   with gratitude.

* * * *

Morning Prayer

Gracious God — and Father of my spirit — as I
waken this morning, let me be aware of my
many mercies.

For a roof over my head during the night — I
bless Thee.

For safe sleep, and the comfort of my bed.

At this customary hour, and in a place so familiar,
I bring Thee my praise!

And as the day opens out, let me be ready to
share the delights of my home, which I have in
plenty.

Help me to use this day well — *and for Thy sake,
I pray*. AMEN.

R.F.S.

An Evening Hymn

We thank Thee then, O Father,
For all things bright and good,
The seed-time and the harvest,
Our life, our health, our food:
Accept the gifts we offer
For all Thy Love imparts,
And what Thou most desirest,
Our humble, thankful hearts.
Matthias Claudius

Stir-up Sunday

HE STIRRETH UP THE PEOPLE (LUKE 23:5; A.V.)

I have in my possession, a *Minister's Manual* where this celebration has its place. And alongside it in my study is "The Book of Common Prayer", where, for the Sunday before Advent, is an entry beginning: *"Stir up, we beseech Thee, O Lord, the wills of Thy faithful people: that they, plenteously bringing forth the fruit of good works, may by Thee be plenteously rewarded, through Jesus Christ our Lord."* It sounds curiously phrased, but to those who give it attention, it adds up to a helpful challenge. Actually, I've never yet been present at a Service of celebration where it has been used. Have you?

Certainly, there are, in our private and congregational experience, times when it could be extremely valuable. Now and again, we are all likely to be overcome by "comfortable casualness" as we go about our daily affairs.

Even Services of worship suffer – it's not every Sunday that we arrive at the church door, and our familiar pew and preacher, full of "holy expectations". Now and again they take us by surprise, as they did John Wesley, when he felt his heart "strangely warmed", and went out to make a much-needed difference to the world about him, both then and for generations following.

But "Stir-up Sunday" can be a simple experience, limited in its ministry, to one or two of us humble people. Yet the new life it brings makes a difference in this Earth-life for evermore. And who today can tell what it may become – if only in the next generation?

There are those "stir-up" experiences, that maybe approach so quietly, richly, invaluably, on the wings of an everyday confidential talk with a long-time friend, that they are hardly counted as holding a spiritual quality. But they do – a transforming, vital reality, a new triumph and joy!

* * * *

Adoration, and Thanksgiving
   O God, it's a wonderful thing to be allowed to live
      on this Earth of Yours –
   With eager, questioning minds,
      and a practical pair of hands –
   With builders, and keepers of beautiful things –
      honest, frank, generous folk —
   Fully alive – true lovers – dreamers of dreams!
                                             R.F.S.

* * * *

Year by year, we find we are being led towards a life too big for this world to contain!
                              The Rev. Dorothy Wilson

Archbishop William Temple, widely-beloved Christian leader, could have been spending time with his well known Book of Common Prayer, even with that part pertaining to "Stir-up Sunday", when he was moved to write: *"If Christianity has never disturbed us, we have not yet learned what it is!"* And when it comes to a discovery worth sharing with everyone, in a book of this sort, it has to come from such an experienced Christian.

Alfred Henry Vine, desiring to share *for life* what had come to him *out of life* in one dark place wrote:

O strangely art Thou with us, Lord,
　Neither in height nor depth to seek;
In nearness shall Thy voice be heard;
　Spirit to spirit Thou dost speak.

Be with us when no other friend
　The mystery of my heart can share;
And be Thou known, when fears transcend,
　By Thy best name of "Comforter".

* * * *

I corresponded continually with a dear Dutch friend as closely as was possible in the dark war days, when hurts and anxieties descended on her family home beside the canal. And when the cessation of hostilities allowed, I went again to that side of the world on my "book interests", and across the Channel to visit my friend (having sent supportive pantry parcels, all the war through). I stayed a few days in her home, and heard many grim and stirring tales of shared hazards. Her greatest single joy was of the wholly wonderful way in which her Faith held!

"What is this quotation?" I asked one day, whilst

handling one of her Dutch books that she loved, being a university lecturer in languages.

"I'll translate it for you," said she. "It means, in English: *'Nobody need walk in darkness, when all around are God's lights!'* "

Though we had both of us, come to peace time, those words still carried an all-important Reality! We dared not relax. This – more than ever, perhaps, because so many of us were so tired – was a time when "Stir-up Sunday" had a special challenge and value!

*　*　*　*

"When you are young," said the late Scottish Christian, Alistair Maclean, in one of his books, "you want to *do* things – to play games, to be happy, to laugh, to dance, to give every dawn an eager welcome, to sing in the sun! When middle years come, you want to *get* things – love, money, promotion, home, children . . . glamorous things. When the westward years appear, you want to *be* things . . . to be large-hearted, tolerant, calm."

*　*　*　*

Charles Wesley's words, in the presence of his God, might well become yours and mine, for here and now:

> Thy sovereign grace to all extends,
>   Immense and unconfined;
> From age to age it never ends;
>   It reaches all mankind.

Throughout the world its breadth is known,
    Wide as infinity;
So wide it never passed by one,
    Or it had passed by me.

                     Charles Wesley

       *   *   *   *

This is your Master – and mine! Utterly to be trusted,
    lastingly, to be loved!
By men and women, of every country, and clime
    Below, and above forever.

                          R.F.S.

       *   *   *   *

Sabatier, in an earlier age, chose to say:

> I can accept no other God and Master than Jesus
>   . . . because in Him alone,
> optimism is without frivolity, and seriousness
>   without despair.

Since early days by Galilee, this is how things have
stood for many. Borrowing Dr Harry Fosdick's
statement:

> In those days when the Master was presenting his
> way of living to the acceptance of men who had
> courage to try it, discipleship was a costly exploit.
> He invited each, *starting where each was.*

And he does still! *What do we say to that?*
   One, in our own day, offers this little Prayer
for use:

Give us the grace to lay at Thy feet our dearest desires and longings, to lay bare before Thee the secret places of our hearts, that all we have, and are, may be Thine to command.   Amen.

Anon

Prayer

Gracious God, I am glad to be alive, and here, well, and awake at this hour.

I bless Thee for the gift of sleep – and now for worthwhile things to *do* – and *be*!

R.F.S.

Thanksgiving

This do I glory in beneath the sun —
    That men and women have lived in evil times,
Have kept glad-hearted under stress of pain,
      Have fought against all odds, and not despaired,
        Have fallen, and died exulting!

Anon

Long ago now, when Columbus raised the flag of Spain over San Salvador and claimed the island for his King, it was important.

Some time later, he returned to the Western hemisphere, and landed at a different spot. Again he raised the flag of Spain, and claimed that piece of territory for his King.

And each time he stepped on to new territory, he did the same!

How good it would be, if you and I could do that. If every time we earned a rise in salary; passed an exam; acquired a new skill; made a new friend; grasped for the first time some larger Christian truth – if every time we did those happy things we lost ourselves utterly, joyously in service for The Kingdom of Christ, how good it would be!

R.F.S.

A Petition in Earnest

Gracious Lord of all I am and achieve; live in my heart, mind and spirit. In all my human relationships; in all my happiest moments; in all my comings and goings – for Christ's sake.   AMEN.

R.F.S.

* * * *

A Psalm at Sunrise

Create in me a clean heart, O God,
    and renew a right spirit within me,
Cast me not away from Thy presence.

Psalm 51:10–11, A.V.

A Psalm at Sundown

It is a good thing to give thanks unto the Lord.

Psalm 92:1; A.V.

Celebrating Closeness

INTERCESSION

Year by year, through my busy, happy writing life, I've paused to do a dedication for the front of a new book, to set there the name of "someone I hold closely in my heart" – and to whom "I owe a debt of gratitude", or "someone to whom I came a stranger, and was received as a friend". Such a reality means a lot on the other side of the world, in the continual travelling I've had to do, and I spend a lot of time, thinking out these dedications, one by one.

I did one lately, for someone whose fresh face I'd never seen, until I went into our city airport, to collect her from among a milling mass. She had written to me many times, from her home, her church and her busy business life on the other side of the world, and now, to my joy, she was on her way to a southern Guide Conference in our beautiful South Island city of Christchurch. I wrote, asking her to phone me as she paused at our airport, going south, and to stop off, on her way back, if she could, to spend a few days with me in my flat. (It could only be a few days, because I was soon to leave for Britain, myself, and certain obligations I had accepted.) It was a lasting experience of heart and mind, and after I had been a guest in her home, over that Easter-tide, and our letters continued, I found myself asking if I might dedicate to her a small devotional book I was doing.

And when a letter reached me bearing her consent, I set about doing that. Such experiences seldom happen in a hurry – but they are God's good gifts, in this Earth life! And my little book – "our" little book – has gone out into a welcoming world, bearing my words: "Dedicated to My Friend Jean, half a world away – *but close*." (It's those last two words, simple, but real, that matter.)

* * * *

In celebrating "Closeness" of any kind that, of course, is what matters. And in our religious life INTER-CESSION is another such important thing. It calls for love and caring, and gentle patience and self-sharing; and a certain knowledge, surely. I doubt whether intercession, which spells "Closeness" of a very special kind, can be a reality without that.

* * * *

Years ago, I wrote of my thoughts at that time, in a book I dedicated:
"To my friend, Dr William Barclay, one of the blessed who *give* without remembering and *receive* without forgetting." (Since the book is now long out of print, alas, and my good friend "gone upon his way", I will repeat here, as a privilege, some of the thoughts that were mine then, on "Intercession", as they have proved *basic*, if at the same time, a little amusing.)

They centred on the little rocky island of St Kilda. I had just come back from a journey, where I'd learned about some happenings there.

Amidst lonely, storm-thrashed seas, St Kilda is relatively small – only three islands and four stacks of volcanic origin, whose greenish-black summits command notice, and are remembered. At the foot of the steep cliffs, the breakers crash into spray. The very largest of the three islands is but six miles in circumference. And that's not very big!

* * * *

So steady has been the required struggle of the people of St Kilda, through the centuries, that one marvels that they ever managed to keep song, laughter, and prayer upon their lips. However, limits are sometimes reached, and in 1930, boats beat their way in, through treacherous seas, and took off all the island folk.

Some idea of their isolation can be glimpsed through an entry in an old diary. In 1830, the Rev. Neil Mackenzie arrived to minister to the lonely people of St Kilda. Some time later, he wrote:

> At the end of this year we heard of the death of William IV; and I was a little horrified to find that I had been praying for him some months after his death. I consequently altered my style of praying, not for anyone by name – but for His Majesty the King. When the packet [ship] came in autumn 1838, I found I was not yet right – and that I should have been praying for Her Majesty the Queen!

Intercession, under those circumstances, must have

always been unsatisfactory.

* * * *

Someone has defined intercession as "Love upon its knees". Very good! But surely it involves more than that – the factual gift of a clear mind, as well, accurate understanding of the situation. Now the problem, in its most acute form, has ceased to trouble the people of St Kilda, though there is a measure in which it can never be resolved for any of our human minds. We are not forced to live on a little storm-girt island – but it does help us, as humans, to *care*, and *love*, and *intercede*, if we understand something of the true nature of things. This is where letters, phone calls, visits, and news in general come in during a crisis situation, making no difference to God's knowledge – but a great difference to our steady, continuing faithfulness in intercession.

Our Master, Jesus, prayed for others, and by name in some cases. There remains no least doubt that a new reality entered into the Master's prayer for Peter, when He prayed for him, as it does into any minister's prayer as he uses his patient's name, when he ministers at his bedside. In the early days of the Church in the world, Paul possessed the same assurance. Unceasingly he wrote to his friends in Rome, to mention only one place. And many are recorded in the New Testament.

* * * *

It is only on rare occasions, I feel, that we can excuse ourselves, along with Janet Pitcairn:

I am too tired to say their names, my Father,
  But Thou dost know
My dear ones. Let them be Thy dear ones,
  And keep them so.

It's not easy to intercede for people – even missionaries, doctors, and nurses – whose names we do not
know, or of whom we never hear a snatch of news.
That is one of the practical, present-moment services
of a good church and missionary magazine. It saves
us from ever "praying for the King, when we ought
to be praying for the Queen".

"Prayer is not", as one has told us very straightly,
"conquering God's reluctance, but taking hold of
God's willingness."

"Intercession," praying for others," says one of our
lively modern writers, Monica Furlong, "is rather
like being a parent who holds up a child above the
heads of the crowd, so that he may see the Queen
go by. The father probably cannot see well himself
. . . he may not see at all. Nevertheless, he can give
the child its chance for a glimpse of glory.

*"Intercession can be compared to holding a person so
that he or she may be exposed to the Love and Beauty of
God!"*

★ ★ ★ ★

"For many years," Dr Mott rejoiced to say, "it has
been my practice, in travelling among the nations,
to make a study of the sources of the spiritual
movements which are doing most to vitalize and
transform individuals, and communities. At times,

it has been difficult to do it, but invariably where I have had the time and patience to do so, I have found it an intercessory prayer life of great reality."

* * * *

Years back, in my youthful shy student days, I came upon a vital truth, in one of Dr Harry Fosdick's little books, one of the first paperbacks I ever handled, which were just then coming into favour. Many who had a limited experience of them were ready to dismiss them as "not *proper* books". But not Dr Fosdick, nor later did Dr William Barclay with his millions of book sales! And I am thankful to God that, in the fullest, most satisfying years of my life's ministry, I have myself had quite a lot to do with paperbacks!

And I'm not unhappy that the first book my present publishers set me to do was a paperback. It had a beautiful jacket – and has now gone into eighteen editions, and into other languages. It was *A Woman's Book of Prayers*, and I am humbled by its unsought foreword by my friend Dr Barclay:

"I have read Miss Snowden's prayers, for the present-day woman with very great interest" wrote he, to my Editor. "It seems to me to answer almost perfectly to its title. The language is modern and yet the language is beautiful. A pattern of prayer is kept all the way through, but what seems to me most important of all is this – there is all through the book an accent of reality. It prays for things which people really want. It thinks in situations which are happening to everyone. It takes the life of every day and lays it before God. And this is precisely what a book like this should do. I am quite sure that this book will make prayer more real and meaningful for all who use it. Here the needs of the twentieth century are brought to God in twentieth-century language, and the everlasting needs are also laid before the throne of grace."

William Barclay

★   ★   ★   ★

Up through the years, many of us have read of the loving example of Forbes Robinson in the matter of praying for others. Recommending the practice to a friend, he wrote:

> Just try to pray for some one person . . . and you will begin really to love him . . . As you lay his life before God, as you pray earnestly for him . . . at the end of the time you will feel more interested in him. You enter into another man's *ego*. You see him *in God*.

★   ★   ★   ★

That is what intercessions means in this life. And it's a pity for any one of us, anywhere, to miss it.

It's true "closeness".

"Deep friendships are rare today," I read in a book, *The Gift of Friends*, by Marion Stroud, with charming, natural illustrations. It was sent to me by my friend

Jean, who intercedes for me on the other side of the world, as I do, daily, for her.

"We have acquaintances and casual friends," it goes on to say, *"but few of us enjoy intimate life-changing relationships that last."*

I wonder if that's true?

Dostoevsky, of an earlier day, wrote strongly: *"To love a person means to see him as God intended him to be."* And this is the test of friendship. Not just to see my friend like that, but to act in such a way that, because we are friends, he will be more able to translate the potential into reality.

Whilst This Life Lasts

A SONG OF HEART AND WHOLENESS

The Christian Faith (have you noticed?) was born, not in a sermon, but in a song. When Christmas came, it was angels, above the shepherds' fields, that met human hearts like ours, with Earth's greatest good news. And in song! I have stood on the rim of those Fields, in Bethlehem, and remembered that heavenly fact. And its wonder lies for ever fresh in my heart! It sends me with joy to the New Testament record of that unexpected happening. Up till then the shepherd men had arranged everything that happened there, as did their fathers before them, and their fathers before them. But this was different, joyously different! There would be many "work experiences" that they would naturally forget with the years – but not this!

Yet there is no set celebration in the Church, to remind us of the event of which they needed no reminding till life's end!

"When you watch religion at work," said Percy Ainsworth, a young English Methodist minister, when I was growing up and trying to think out my discipleship, "you see a mortality; when you think deeply about it, you find a theology but when you come to the very heart of it, you find *a song!*" Dr Luke rejoiced to record it:

And there were in the same country shepherds abiding in the field, keeping watch over their flock by night. And, lo, the angel of the Lord came upon them, and the glory of the Lord shone round about them; and they were sore afraid. And the angel said unto them, "Fear not: for behold, I bring you good tidings of great joy, which shall be to all people. For unto you is born this day in the city of David, a Saviour, which is Christ the Lord. And this shall be a sign unto you. Ye shall find the babe wrapped in swaddling clothes, lying in a manger."

And suddenly there was with the angel, a multitude of the heavenly host praising God, and saying, "Glory to God in the highest, and on earth peace, good will toward men."

And it came to pass, as the angels were gone away from them into heaven, the shepherds said one to another, "Let us now go even unto Bethlehem, and see this thing which is come to pass, which the Lord hath made known unto us. And they came with haste, and found Mary, and Joseph, and the babe lying in a manger. And when they had seen it, they made known abroad the saying which was told them concerning this child. And all they that heard it wondered at these things which were told them by the shepherds.

But Mary kept all these things, and pondered them in her heart.

Luke 2:8–19; A.V.

* * * *

Christmas – and Always

In the first Christian century, Pliny was an interested listener to the place that song held amongst members of the "new sect", as Christianity then was. It wasn't that for them life was always easy – not at all.

But they continued to assemble, despite all manner of dangers in the dark streets they dared to use. The remarkable thing was that somehow, in their little meetings, "they kept singing", as others did not. Hymns to Christ as God – despite what had happened to Him on the Cross. But for all that, they had something to sing about! Their Lord, they believed, as did their two compatriots, after their close experience on the way home to Emmaus, was alive! He had talked with them, walked with them, and at sundown – tired, their three shadows long-stretched-out on the dusty roadway – had accepted their invitation, and gone in to share a meal with them. After that moment, when they saw and recognized the way He handled things, there was never the slightest doubt: *He was alive!*

And soon, the Christians back in Jerusalem were sharing that belief. There was a lot to sing about! Then in the second century, Clement of Alexandria had much the same remarkable story to tell. With gladness, he related the issuing of Christian faith in song – not only in the place of worship, hidden away in some home in a back street; but also in the place of work. He wrote: "Holding festival, then, in our whole life, we cultivate our fields, praising; we sail the sea, hymning; in all the rest of our conversation we conduct ourselves according to rule."

* * * *

Jerome, centuries on, had the same glad stories to tell: "The ploughman at his plough sings his joyful hallelujahs; the busy mower refreshes himself with psalms; the vinedresser sings the songs of David." "All come together with us to sing," adds Chrysostom later, "and in it they unitedly join, the young and the old, the rich and the poor; women and men, slaves and free; all send forth one melody."

★　★　★　★

So the faith in which men and women lived and died comes down to us "on wings of song", helped, of course, by the great hymnwriters, many of them known to us by name. They included the Wesley brothers, and many since, men and women, God be praised! As time moves on, this rich heritage of song supports our ongoing Christian Faith, and beautifies it!

So our modern poet, Lascelles Abercrombie, likes to pass on the four-line challenge, that we dare not leave un-accepted.

Crumble, crumble,
Voiceless things.
No Faith can last,
That never sings!

★　★　★　★

It is not often, if ever, that we think of Jesus singing, but if we turn toward the end of Mark's little gospel, the first of them all, there is a simple verse, which, once we think of it, we shall never pass by again.

(Mark 14:26). Don't expect it to be a jolly song, as when a man and his friends gather together for a last meal. It was a solemn occasion. Mark wrote of it: *"And when they had sung an hymn, they went out into the mount of Olives."* (By this, they all knew what that could mean.) He told them more, and Mark wrote it down. "But Peter said unto him, Although all shall be offended, yet will not I. And Jesus saith unto him, Verily I say unto thee, That this day, even in this night, before the cock crow twice, thou shalt deny me thrice." . . . It was not an easy occasion. If you've ever wondered about that "hymn", the expositor, Dr Halford E. Luccock, wrote of it:

Those who stand completely outside the experience of worship, and they are many, disdain it. And empty worship, God help us all, can indeed, be the veriest vanity. But for Jesus and His disciples this singing of a hymn was no mere form. There may have been wavering voices at first, but as they shared in Israel's great religious heritage of faith, they found a power arming their minds and hearts against whatever might be waiting for them. When they had sung a hymn they were renewed men, with spirits replenished in a fellowship of worship with each other and with the great company who had sung the same hymn in days gone by . . .

That is what worship can do. It is not an entertainment or an aesthetic diversion. It is a fortifying power. The great scenes of Christian history might bear these words as a subtitle: "When they had sung a hymn, they went out." It was true of the martyrs as they went into the amphitheatre to face the lions. It was true of the early leaders of the anti-slavery movements; it has been true of thousands of fare-well meetings for departing missionaries. It was true of Norwegian churchmen defying the Nazi tyranny.

What is true of us?

Is it true that we do not "go out" more effec-tively in the conflict with evil, because we do not worship effectively enough? Is it true that after we have sung a hymn, we all too often sit down instead of going out at all? The hymns we sing and the prayers we offer have to take deep inward hold if there is to be any projection outward.

The Interpreter's Bible:
Mark, p. 879; Dr Halford E. Luccock

Prayer for the Day
Gracious God, our Father, in Whose hands are the issues of life and outreaching service, let our offering this day be acceptable in Thy sight. Thou hast set us to live here among men and women, and little children, and by deeds, more than words, to make real to teenagers the values of Thy lasting Kingdom. Save us from ever keeping our religion a secretive, private possession. And deliver us from being wholly solemn – set some laughter upon our tongues as we share our work, and our play. And amid the serious things with which we must deal, some *song!*

Keep alive in our hearts and minds a continual concern for those about us. They are not all our types, our friends, or in any way closely linked to our daily lives. But when work, sport or travel throws us together, let us show them a kindly respect – and be ready with what help we can give them. And save us from any pride, or seeming superiority. For Christ's sake.   AMEN.

R.F.S.

My song is love unknown;
My Saviour's love to me;
Love to the loveless shown,
That they might lovely be.
O who am I,
That for my sake
My Lord should take
Frail flesh, and die?

Sometimes they strew His way,
And His sweet praises sing;
Resounding all the day
Hosannas to their King.
Then "Crucify!"
Is all their breath,
And for His death
They thirst and cry.

Here might I stay and sing,
No story so divine;
Never was love, dear King,
Never was grief like Thine.
This is my Friend,
In whose sweet praise

Whilst This Life Lasts

I all my days
Could gladly spend.

Samuel Crossman

ACKNOWLEDGEMENTS

The author acknowledges with gratitude the use of the following material:

T. S. Eliot, "Journey of the Magi" from *Collected Poems*, Faber & Faber, London, 1909.

Eleanor Farjeon, "Morning Has Broken" from *The Children's Bells*, Oxford University Press; used by permission of David Higham Associates, Ltd, London.

Gerard Manley Hopkins, "Nothing is so Beautiful" from *Poems by Gerard Manley Hopkins*, ed. Norman H. Mackenzie, Folio, London, 1974.

G. A. Studdert-Kennedy, "And Sitting Down . . ." poem from *Collected Poems*, Hodder & Stoughton, London.

All other extracts are used with the direct permission of the authors. In rare cases the author has been unable to trace the current copyright holder, but such sources will be acknowledged in any future reprint of this volume, if further information comes to hand.

Also available in Fount Paperbacks

The Mind of St Paul
WILLIAM BARCLAY

'There is a deceptive simplicity about this fine exposition of Pauline thought at once popular and deeply theological. The Hebrew and Greek backgrounds are described and all the main themes are lightly but fully treated.'   *The Yorkshire Post*

The Plain Man Looks at the Beatitudes
WILLIAM BARCLAY

'. . . the author's easy style should render it . . . valuable and acceptable to the ordinary reader.'   *Church Times*

The Plain Man Looks at the Lord's Prayer
WILLIAM BARCLAY

Professor Barclay shows how this prayer that Jesus gave to his disciples is at once a summary of Christian teaching and a pattern for all prayers.

The Plain Man's Guide to Ethics
WILLIAM BARCLAY

The author demonstrates beyond all possible doubt that the Ten Commandments are the most relevant document in the world today and are totally related to mankind's capacity to live and make sense of it all within a Christian context.

Ethics in a Permissive Society
WILLIAM BARCLAY

How do we as Christians deal with such problems as drug taking, the 'pill', alcohol, morality of all kinds, in a society whose members are often ignorant of the Church's teaching? Professor Barclay approaches a difficult and vexed question with his usual humanity and clarity, asking what Christ himself would say or do in our world today.

Also available in Fount Paperbacks

The Holy Spirit
BILLY GRAHAM

'This is far and away Graham's best book. It bears the stamp of someone who has seen everything, and then has worked painstakingly and carefully in making his own assessment . . . The Christian world will be reading it for many years to come.'

Richard Bewes,
Church of England Newspaper

To Live Again
CATHERINE MARSHALL

The moving story of one woman's heart-rending grief and of her long hard struggle to rediscovery of herself, of life, of hope.

A Man Called Peter
CATHERINE MARSHALL

The story of a brilliantly successful minister and of a dynamic personality. Told by his wife, it is also the story of their life together; a record of love and faith that has few equals in real life.

The Prayer's of Peter Marshall
CATHERINE MARSHALL

'This is a truly wonderful book, for these prayers are a man speaking to God – and speaking in a way that involves listening for an answer.'   *British Weekly*

I Believe
Trevor Huddleston

A simple, prayerful series of reflections on the phrases of the Creed. This is a beautiful testament of the strong, quiet inner faith of a man best known for his active role in the Church – and in the world.

The Heart of the Christian Faith
Donald Coggan

The author ". . . presents the essential core of Christianity in a marvellously simple and readable form, quite uncluttered by any excess of theological technicality."
The Yorkshire Post

Be Still and Know
Michael Ramsey

The former Archbishop of Canterbury looks at prayer in the New Testament, at what the early mystics could teach us about it, and at some practical aspects of Christian praying.

Pilgrim's Progress
John Bunyan

"A masterpiece which generation after generation of ordinary men and women have taken to their hearts."
Hugh Ross Williamson

Fount Paperbacks

Fount is one of the leading paperback publishers of religious books and below are some of its recent titles.

- [ ] FRIENDSHIP WITH GOD David Hope £2.95
- [ ] THE DARK FACE OF REALITY Martin Israel £2.95
- [ ] LIVING WITH CONTRADICTION Esther de Waal £2.95
- [ ] FROM EAST TO WEST Brigid Marlin £3.95
- [ ] GUIDE TO THE HERE AND HEREAFTER
  Lionel Blue/Jonathan Magonet £4.50
- [ ] CHRISTIAN ENGLAND (1 Vol) David Edwards £10.95
- [ ] MASTERING SADHANA Carlos Valles £3.95
- [ ] THE GREAT GOD ROBBERY George Carey £2.95
- [ ] CALLED TO ACTION Fran Beckett £2.95
- [ ] TENSIONS Harry Williams £2.50
- [ ] CONVERSION Malcolm Muggeridge £2.95
- [ ] INVISIBLE NETWORK Frank Wright £2.95
- [ ] THE DANCE OF LOVE Stephen Verney £3.95
- [ ] THANK YOU, PADRE Joan Clifford £2.50
- [ ] LIGHT AND LIFE Grazyna Sikorska £2.95
- [ ] CELEBRATION Margaret Spufford £2.95
- [ ] GOODNIGHT LORD Georgette Butcher £2.95
- [ ] GROWING OLDER Una Kroll £2.95

All Fount Paperbacks are available at your bookshop or newsagent, or they can be ordered by post from Fount Paperbacks, Cash Sales Department, G.P.O. Box 29, Douglas, Isle of Man. Please send purchase price plus 22p per book, maximum postage £3. Customers outside the UK send purchase price, plus 22p per book. Cheque, postal order or money order. No currency.

NAME (Block letters) _____

ADDRESS_____

_____

_____